Also available from Continuum

Sue Cowley: *Getting the Buggers to Behave*
Angela Thody et al.: *Teacher's Survial Guide*

Starting Teaching
How to Succeed and Survive

Sue Cowley

CONTINUUM

London and New York

Continuum

The Tower Building, 11 York Road, London SE1 7NX
370 Lexington Avenue, New York NY10017-6503
www.continuumbooks.com

First published 1999 by Cassell
Reprinted 2001 by Continuum

British Library Cataloguing-in-Publication Data
A catalogue record for this book is available from the British Library.

ISBN 0-8264-5108-X

Typeset by York House Typographic Ltd., London
Printed and bound in Great Britain by Bookcraft, Midsomer Norton.

Contents

This book is dedicated to all the
teachers, students, friends and loved ones
who helped me succeed in, survive and enjoy
my first teaching job.

Acknowledgements

Special thanks go to the following people for their support, encouragement, friendship and inspiration: the staff at Drayton Manor High School, especially John Rust-Andrews, Linda Huntley, John Browning, David Henderson, Simon Horne, Caroline Evernden, Luan Binnion, Jenny Burn, Chris Everall and Kate McClean; all my teachers at Kingston University; Elka Giemza, Tim and Veronique Charman, Adrian Crilly, Michelle Newton, Alison Cowley and Bernard Cowley.

Extra special thanks and love go to my Mum and to Tilak Castellino, for making it all possible.

Introduction

So, you've worked long and hard to qualify as a teacher, after endless form filling and interviews you've found yourself a job, and now it's time to put it all into practice. But how ready do you actually feel to stand in front of a class and teach? And how do you deal with all the other aspects of a real teaching job? Somehow, that's something they forgot to tell you at college. Well, that's what this book is designed to show you.

Before I trained as a teacher, I worked in a variety of 'real' jobs – jobs where, if the clients didn't like what your firm was doing, they simply took their money elsewhere. But it doesn't work like that in education. When I started teaching I was amazed to find out just how inefficient schools can be: how much time is wasted on inessential, administrative tasks; how many pieces of (often unnecessary) paper pass through your hands in an average week; how disciplined you have to be to spend your time in the most effective way.

In teaching, you are your own boss, and this is perhaps one of the main attractions of the profession. However, the job will expand to meet the amount of time you are willing to devote to it, and this means that you will have to develop self-discipline and time management skills if you are not going to be working until midnight every night! There are so many things about teaching you can only learn 'on the job'. You will have to find ways to deal with problem students and awkward parents; decide how much time you can really afford to spend on marking; develop a teaching style that works for all your students and so on.

I can remember feeling completely 'at sea' in my first year of teaching, adrift without any certainties to anchor on to, drowning in a sea of paperwork. This book contains answers to all the questions I had and will give you guidance in overcoming some of the obstacles that stand in your way. This is *not* an academic textbook based on years of painstaking research. It is full of common-sense advice, based on my own experiences as a teacher. I have tried to combine practical tips with examples (sometimes light-hearted) to help you succeed and survive as you start out on your teaching career.

Although I work as a secondary school teacher, I actually trained to teach young children, and I am constantly surprised at how similar students of all different ages are. Many of the techniques that I used with 3-year-olds are applicable to 18-year-olds as well! So, although this book is written from the perspective of a secondary school teacher, it is actually aimed at *all* teachers, whatever age range they are teaching.

I would like to wish you luck in your prospective profession – you have chosen one of the most varied, interesting and rewarding jobs it is possible to find. You have also chosen a career that is exhausting, often incredibly hard work and which may well reduce you to tears. However, if you find that teaching is the job for you, you will be entering a worthwhile and rewarding career in which you will be able to make a real difference to your students. And with time and dedication you may become the most important type of teacher: a teacher that they will never forget.

Part I

Getting Started

Chapter 1

Survival Tactics

BEFORE YOU START

Whatever you do, do not succumb to the temptation to spend the summer planning wonderful and exciting schemes of work, as you were taught to do at college. Although you may believe that you are saving yourself time, you will probably discover that any detailed planning done at this stage is fairly meaningless. Until you meet your students and get to know them a little, it is hard to anticipate their needs and interests. You may have received your timetable and information about your classes, but there could be changes made that you only discover when you actually start work at the school. It is also likely that some (or all) of your teaching will be dictated by the schemes of work and textbooks being used in your department.

If you are given the opportunity, do go and visit the school during the spring or summer term. Although you will have been shown around the school on the day you were interviewed, it is worth while taking another look when you are not feeling quite so tense. Remember that at this time of year examination students will probably be on study leave, and this can make a substantial difference to the appearance and feel of a school. The best advice, of course, is to take a long and relaxing holiday, although whether your finances will be up to this is another matter.

THE FIRST DAY

In reality you will have two 'first' days: a 'training day' (or perhaps two or three training days) when all the staff return to school and the actual 'start of term', when the students arrive.

The training day

Your first training day may feel like an intimidating affair. The staff will probably be gathered in the staff room, chatting away to each other, discussing all the exciting things they did over the summer. You, of course, will know only one or two people from your interview, possibly the headteacher and perhaps the head of your department. Probably the two people you least want to socialize with.

It is highly unlikely that the staff will dress smartly on the training day. In most cases it is acceptable to dress casually, although if you feel uncomfortable doing this you could dress 'smart casual'. The embarrassment of wearing a suit when everyone else is in jeans is something you could do without at this stage, especially if you are asked to stand up to be introduced to the rest of the staff!

Schools use their 'training days' in a variety of different ways. In some schools the teachers are given lots of freedom to prepare for when the students return; in others the time is strictly allocated, with a number of different meetings being scheduled. It is likely that there will be a full staff meeting at some stage, in which the head will welcome everyone back, explain any promotions that have taken place and introduce the new teachers (including you). There may also be various administrative and whole-school issues to deal with, for instance if your school is scheduled for an inspection.

You may well have a departmental meeting on your training day or days and again there will be lots of administration to do – sorting books, checking deliveries and so on. If you are allocated preparation or departmental time this gives you the perfect opportunity to become acquainted with the other members of your department or those working near to you. Even if you are the most confident individual in the world, it is probably worth keeping fairly quiet at this stage to avoid making the wrong impression. You should ensure that you collect the various papers you will need. These include:

- a 'teacher's planner' (if your school uses them) – see Chapter 2
- the finalized copy of your timetable
- your class lists
- copies of schemes of work and syllabuses (if possible)
- sets of books or textbooks you will be teaching
- exercise books and paper (if they are available).

When you receive all these papers, it is very tempting to start organizing them immediately: sticking your timetable and class lists into your planner, writing out your first week's lessons, and so on. Do try to avoid this temptation. The first week of school never runs quite according to the timetable – for instance on the first day back the students may have year assemblies and registration or 'tutor' time. Class lists, too, are often subject to change when new students join the school or others do not turn up. Simply keep all your important papers in a folder to deal with at a later stage.

Some schools have problems with a lack of space, and teachers are forced to move around from classroom to classroom for their different lessons. However, if you are lucky you may be given a 'room of your own' to work in and you could spend a little time before the students arrive stamping your personality on it – perhaps putting up a 'welcome' notice with your name on it. This will give your students the impression that you know what you are doing and it will also save you from having your name spelt wrongly.

Try to collect all the resources you may need now, so that you are fully prepared for when the students arrive. Exercise books and paper can be like gold dust at the start of term, especially if orders have not yet been delivered. If you have a form group, you will also need to collect diaries, timetables and other items for them (see Chapter 5 for more information on this).

One of the greatest difficulties you will face at first is finding your way around the building. If at all possible before the students arrive spend some time walking around the school, preferably with someone who knows their way around. It is useful to know the location of the following:

- the school office
- the student reception, if there is one
- the head's office
- the deputy head's office
- the offices of senior staff, e.g. heads of year or house
- photocopying machines
- the assembly hall
- the caretaker's office
- the staff toilets!

The start of term

So here it is at last, the moment you have been waiting for. Your stomach feels like lead, you are convinced you are going to be sick and your mouth is as dry as the Sahara Desert. Even the most experienced teachers find the start of term difficult. How on earth are you supposed to deal with it?

Chapter 3 gives you lots of hints on classroom management, but at this point I'd like to offer you a few tips and thoughts that might help you through this terrifying (and I'm not exaggerating) experience:

1. *You are 'the mystery teacher'* No one knows who you are yet. They may suspect that you are inexperienced, but unless you tell them, or give the impression of being scared, they have no way of knowing for sure. At the moment you are an unknown quantity and consequently you have an air of mystery around you that you can exploit.

   If a student asks you the question 'Are you a new teacher, Miss/Sir?' simply answer, 'I'm new to this school.' At the same time, try to cultivate the sense that you have a wealth of experience behind you, teaching or otherwise. No matter how inexperienced *you* are, the students are always less experienced (and younger).

2. *'They're more scared of you …'* You know the old saying about spiders and snakes: *'They're more scared of you than you are of them.'* This saying also holds true for your students. Every teacher has a window of opportunity in which to prove themselves to any class, a few lessons during which the students are still 'checking you out' and are unsure just how far they can push you.

   Think very carefully about your teaching style before you start. The old cliché that you were probably taught at college actually contains a lot of truth: '*Start off by being as "hard" as possible, you can always relax, but you can never get a class back once you've lost them.*' You are not their friend, mother/father figure or counsellor, you are their teacher, and they will expect and indeed *want* a certain degree of formality. I am not saying that you should scare the living daylights out of them, but do be as strict as you can.

Once you become more experienced as a teacher, and indeed once you get to know your classes during the year, you may well be able to relax. However, if you start 'soft' you are laying down trouble for yourself in the future. Honestly.

3. *Set the boundaries now*   At this stage the name of the game is setting boundaries, letting the students know exactly what you expect of them (and why), what will happen to them if they do not follow your rules, and the rewards that they can expect if they do. Your boundaries should be fair, realistic and achievable. Talk to your classes about what you want and why you want it. Encourage them to respond to your ideas. This will help them feel more secure about how they should behave.

The problem for you at this stage is deciding what your boundaries are going to be. Your school will probably have a set of 'classroom rules', but these may be rather vague. What you need the students to understand is exactly how you want them to behave. To a large extent this is a matter of personal taste and opinion. It also depends a great deal on the type of students you have to teach. After a few years of teaching you will have made decisions about your own expectations but Chapter 3 gives some examples of boundaries, sanctions and rewards I would set for a class to help you at this point. Some schools ask you to 'negotiate' classroom behaviour, but generally this translates as the teacher moulding the students' ideas to their own.

4. *Wait for them*   In Chapter 3 I cover this idea in more detail, but it bears repeating a million times, and is never more important than on your first day with the students. Even the proverbial 'class from hell' will listen to you the first time they meet you. If you set the standard now, they will know what you expect. So, keep this in mind: *never, ever talk to a class until every single student is sitting still, in complete silence and looking directly at you.* The seconds while you are waiting can seem like hours at first, but set this pattern of behaviour now and I promise you that you won't regret it. Even if you find it difficult at first to utilize the rest of the ideas in this book, keep this one thought in your mind when you start out on your teaching career.

5. *Hands up!*   Start every question with the phrase, 'Put your hand up if you can tell me … '. This avoids the irritation of students calling out the answers and after a while you will have trained them to respond to every question by raising their hands.

6. *Relax*   As difficult as it may sound, it is important for your own sake, and for that of the students, not to rush your first lessons. Try to relax, and never worry if there are pauses while you are considering what you want to do next. After a while it will come more easily to you.

7. *Admin, admin, admin, names*   Bear in mind that there are a lot of administrative tasks to complete in the first few lessons that you spend with any class. Checking registers, giving out books and so on will take a great deal of time. Don't feel the

need to rush into your curriculum. You need to learn the students' names as quickly as possible and you will also be finding out about their behaviour and how they work. Chapters 3 and 9 give much more information on this.

8. *Use the register* Although it may seem relatively unimportant at this stage, do get into the habit of taking the register for every class you teach. When you come to write reports, you will need to know how good a student's level of attendance is. Taking the register will also tell you who owes homework and allow you to check for truancy. Above all, the register is an excellent method of control. If used at the beginning of the lesson it settles the class down, prepares them for the lesson, and you can mark as late anyone who arrives after the register.

9. *Who wants a job?* Always, always ask this question when you have anything you want given out or collected in. You will find that your students are delighted to help you (especially the younger ones) and you will save yourself unnecessary work. You can even use this as a 'reward' if your class is keen. The same idea applies for collecting the register to bring to you at form registration time, although do make sure you choose someone reliable for this important job.

10. *Stand behind your chairs* This may sound like a rather minor matter to be worried about when you have a million other difficulties to contend with. However, I promise you it is a worthwhile (and very simple) exercise which will help you control your class and also save you a great deal of time and effort. At the end of the lesson or the day, just before the bell or buzzer goes, ask your students to stand behind their chairs and wait for you to dismiss them. By doing this you have their attention in case you need to give them any instructions or reminders, you can walk around and check that there is no litter on the floor and you have saved yourself the job of pushing in the chairs! Once you have set this pattern, you will find that the students stand behind their chairs automatically.

An extension of this idea is to turn the exercise into a 'game' for younger students. Tell them that they are being 'tested' on how quietly they can stand behind their chairs. This makes the end of the lesson nice and restful for you, as it avoids scraping chairs (and much quieter for the teacher of the class below you if you are on the first floor). A further extension is to then tell the students they must 'freeze' as if they are statues until the buzzer goes. You could give rewards for this to encourage them, for instance allowing the 'best' students to leave first.

THE FIRST WEEK

By the end of the first week you will (hopefully) be finding your feet. You will have faced each of your classes at least once. You will have an idea of what your timetable is like and the structure of your days. At this stage, try to gain an overview of the balance of your week. There may be days when all your lessons are 'heavy' or 'teacher-intensive', but other days when you have a fairly 'light' timetable. Try and account for this variety in your planning. Do not plan whole days of lessons where you will be doing a lot of talking. Allocate some marking time so that you do not set too much work or fall too far behind. Chapters 2 and 7 on planning and marking cover these aspects in much more detail.

DEVELOPING SUPPORT SYSTEMS

Whatever job you do it is important to have someone to turn to for help: a shoulder to cry on when things are going wrong; someone to ask when you need advice or information; people to support you if others question your work. In teaching these support systems are absolutely vital. Teaching is a very difficult job and you will be put in situations where you are challenged in many different ways: physically, emotionally and even legally.

So, start thinking about developing your own support systems as a teacher as soon as possible, preferably *before* you actually need to use them! Support systems for teachers come in a variety of forms: which one you turn to will depend on the type of problem you are experiencing:

1. *Your teaching colleagues*   You will probably find that there are surprisingly few opportunities for you to meet with other teachers, particularly if you are working in a large school. Obviously you will have contact with those who work near you, and with other members of your department, but the majority of each day will be spent with your students. Although it can seem a lot of trouble for a quick cup of coffee, it is worth trying to make time to visit the staff room on your breaks. Not only will you get the chance to chat to other teachers, but you will also give yourself a well-deserved rest from the students.

    As soon as possible, preferably at the end of the first week, try to get involved in any social activities that are taking place (for instance a game of football or netball, going out for a drink). One of the best resources in any school is its teachers and their experience. Once you get to know them a little, you can ask other members of staff for advice, for information, for a copy of that excellent scheme of work. You may also get a chance to moan or cry on a sympathetic shoulder. Your colleagues are a vital part of your support system: get to know them quickly.

2. *Your mentor*   Many schools now run a system whereby newly qualified teachers are given a 'mentor' – an experienced teacher who guides them through their first year, watching them at work and assessing their progress. If you are allocated a mentor, they will become a vital part of your support system, particularly if you find that you get on well with them. More information about mentoring can be found in Chapter 15.

3. *Your head of department*   Your head of department is responsible for all the members of staff in their subject area. They have responsibility for what is taught and how it is delivered. They will also deal with any parent or student comments (good or bad) about your work. It is a excellent idea, both on a professional and a personal level, to develop a good relationship with your head of department. A good head of department will support you in times of need and will also help you to develop your career in the direction you want.

4. *Non-teaching members of staff*   There are a variety of people working in any school who are not actually on the teaching staff: caretakers, receptionists, secretaries, accounting staff, and so on. If you take the time to get to know them, you will find that they can help you out in many different ways. They will be able to make life much easier for you: smoothing your path when you want to arrange a trip; moving furniture for you at short notice; accessing computerized informa-

tion; typing letters, and so on. More information on getting to know the right people is given in Chapter 10.

5. *Teaching unions*   While there is no compulsion for teachers to join a union, there are many advantages in doing so, and a union can form a vital part of your support systems. An important advantage of belonging to a union is the technical advice and support on legal and contractual issues that they offer. With all the stresses of starting work as a teacher, it can be very helpful to gain straightforward advice on such matters. As a new member of staff you may feel uncomfortable approaching a more senior teacher with these questions: a union representative can offer you non-partisan advice.

Details about each union and the main benefits they offer are given below, along with any particular standpoints that may attract you to an organization. Membership of all the unions is free to student teachers. Subscription rates for each union change from year to year, and more detail on these can be obtained by contacting the unions: addresses and contact numbers are given in the Appendix.

The Association of Teachers and Lecturers (ATL)

The ATL has more than 150,000 members. Membership is free for newly qualified teachers in the autumn term and is 50 per cent of the normal rate for the first two years of teaching. The benefits of joining the ATL include free advice and guidance on a range of professional issues; expert legal advice and representation; access to 24-hour helplines; many useful publications; automatic insurance for school-related accidents; and a range of discounted insurance and financial offers.

The ATL provides two services specifically for newly qualified teachers: a dedicated helpline and an annual 'Forum' for new teachers from around the country. Members receive the ATL Report eight times a year and also 'Up-Date', a monthly news bulletin. Free publications available to members include *Managing Classroom Behaviour* and *School Teachers' Conditions of Employment*. The ATL has no political affiliations and is the only teachers' union to have national negotiating rights in primary, secondary and further education. Full membership of the union is not open to headteachers or principals. The ATL never instructs members to follow a particular line of action: for instance, if industrial action was approved after a ballot, members would not have to take part.

The National Association of Schoolmasters and Union of Women Teachers (NASUWT)

The NASUWT has 168,000 members. Membership of the union is free to newly qualified teachers during the autumn term, and to those on temporary/supply contracts. The first two years of membership are at 50 per cent of the full rate. Among the benefits offered by the union are: full professional and legal advice, support and representation in all teaching-related matters; the opportunity to apply for assistance from the NASUWT Benevolent Fund; free insurance cover for school-related incidents; and a number of discounted insurance and financial benefits.

Members receive a free termly journal and the association's newspaper. There are also a lot of free booklets, pamphlets and manuals available including: *Your Teaching Career: Salaries of Newly Qualified Teachers*, *Conditions of Service: A Guide for Students and New Teachers* and *Training to Teach*. The NASUWT has policies on conditions of service, salaries, equal opportunities, and also campaigns to stop personal harrassment in schools and colleges. The union believes that newly qualified teachers should have a reduced timetable. The NASUWT is totally independent and has no political affiliations.

The National Union of Teachers (NUT)

The NUT has over 276,000 members. Membership of the union is free to newly qualified teachers during the autumn term and at half price for the next two years. Other reduced rates are available for teachers on part-time, supply and fixed-term contracts. Benefits of membership include: free insurance for school-related matters; access to professional support and legal protection; an extensive training programme; and a number of specially negotiated deals, including insurance, travel and motoring. Members receive a 'countdown card' which gives them access to many discounted services.

The NUT's publications include *The Teacher*, a colour magazine sent free to all members. Other free publications include: *Teachers' Guide to the Profession*, *Your Passport to Teaching* and *Obtaining Your First Teaching Post*. The NUT also runs a 24-hour 'Crime and Accident' helpline for members. The NUT is the oldest teaching union and has a long tradition of campaigning for equal opportunities. It is currently campaigning for proper induction for newly qualified teachers. The union is in favour of one organization to represent all teachers. The NUT has no political affiliations.

The Professional Association of Teachers (PAT)

The PAT has around 36,000 members. Membership is free to newly qualified teachers during the autumn term and at a reduced rate during the first two years of teaching. Membership is available on a termly basis for those on fixed-term contracts. Benefits of membership include: free professional and legal advice on teaching-related issues; a national network of trained field officers; and a number of free insurance benefits and discounts from various companies.

The union publishes three different free journals, aimed at different sectors of the teaching profession: *Professional Teacher*, *Professional Lecturer* and *Professional Nursery Nurse*. Members also receive a free handbook. There are many free factsheets available including *Preparing for Teaching Practice and Beyond* and *Obtaining Your First Post in Teaching*. The union campaigns about educational and pay and conditions issues on a local and national level. The PAT is independent and strictly non-party political. To join PAT you must agree not to go on strike under any circumstances.

THE FIRST TERM: SEPTEMBER TO DECEMBER

Your first term at a school will be a busy and exciting time. As you get to know the students and find your way around the school you will start to grow in confidence. Half-term will seem to arrive very quickly and your workload may even seem manageable at this stage! This term is full of fun and excitement in the build-up to Christmas: there will probably be lots of events going on and you should really be able to enjoy yourself. There are, however, a few points to be aware of at this stage:

1. *Overconfidence*   Do be careful not to become overconfident and relax with your classes too early. Your students may be responding well to the boundaries that you have set, but if you allow your standards to slip now they may lapse into poor behaviour. Remember that you will have to face your students again after Christmas, when the end of the school year suddenly seems very far away and everyone gets tired and despondent.
2. *Extra activities*   Beware of becoming involved with lots of extra activities: the Christmas concert, the school play, working parties, the Parent–Teacher Association (PTA) and so on. It is very tempting when you start teaching to join in anything and everything to make a good impression. The other reason you may find yourself over-involved is that the older (more cynical, sensible or experienced) members of staff have developed the ability to refuse demands on their time. You may find it hard to refuse to take part if someone asks you to.
3. *Illness/exhaustion/stress*   You want to keep going, to prove to your school that you are a reliable, hard-working employee. So, when you catch flu you muddle through and then wonder why you can't shift the succession of colds that follow. Teachers are notorious for going to work when they should be at home in bed with a lemsip. 'My classes need me', they say, 'I'll only have twice as much work to do when I get back.' I know teachers who keep going and going and then every holiday, without fail, they fall ill.

   A few points for you to think about on this one. Are you really so irreplaceable or important that the school cannot do without you for one or two days? Do you really want to pass on the flu to all the other teachers at your school? Isn't it better to take a day off now and then when you need it, rather than two weeks off when you finally realize that you just can't keep going any longer?

   When you do need to take time off sick, make sure you follow your school 'policy', which will probably involve telephoning to notify them of your absence, the reason you are away, and your likely return date. You may well have to phone in for every day you are absent. You will also need to speak to a member of your department to set work and 'sign in' on the day you return to school.
4. *Evaluation*   If you are a newly qualified teacher your progress will be officially evaluated and some of your lessons will be appraised. Chapter 15 provides details of the mentoring and appraisal process. However, it is also worth getting into the habit of self-evaluation, as this is one of the best, quickest and most readily available ways of improving your teaching.

   If one of your lessons goes particularly well, take a few minutes just to think about what it was that made this lesson work, so that you can repeat it in the future. Similarly, if a strategy that you adopt doesn't work, or if you find yourself in a confrontation with one of your students, think about why this happened and how you might stop yourself repeating the mistake.

THE SECOND TERM: JANUARY TO APRIL

Any teacher will tell you that the second term of the school year is the hardest. The days are short, dark and cold (especially difficult if you teach physical education). The staff are tired and run down, and waves of illness spread through the school like wildfire, hitting both the teachers and the students. Spring and summer seem ages away and the rest of the school year stretches ahead of you like a prison sentence. You have a terrible hangover from Christmas and the New Year. The paperwork is starting to pile up and you are wondering whether you made the wrong career choice.

This is the stage of the school year when you really do just have to grin and bear it. One useful tip, however, is to think about using the February half-term for a holiday. Don't take any work with you, escape somewhere relaxing and warm, and when your students receive an exotic postcard they will be impressed. If you do stay at home, you will no doubt end up working throughout your break, trying to dig through that pile of paper that has somehow appeared on your desk. (See Chapter 6 for some ideas on dealing with paperwork.)

THE THIRD TERM: MAY TO JULY

At last! The end of the year is in sight. The third term always comes as a relief and is often a very enjoyable time. Examinations will be taking place, with some students on study leave, hopefully giving you some extra free time. Although your marking load could become quite heavy, you will be amazed at how the word 'exam' turns your students into silent and hard-working young people.

Now is the time to relax and enjoy your teaching. A lot of schools have their sports day during this term, and it can be very enlightening to see some of your 'worst' or academically weakest students achieving excellent results on the sports field. One word of warning: hot weather can create a sense of lethargy, both in you and in your students. It is up to you whether you decide to crack the whip, or (if you are allowed) to do all your lessons outdoors.

Chapter 2

Planning

THE TEACHER'S PLANNER

If your school uses them, the 'teacher's planner' is a very useful way of keeping all your important information in one place. The planner is basically a small (A5 size) or large (A4 size) book in which you can keep all (or most of) the information you would have kept in your teaching practice file during your training. It will probably contain the following sections:

- a yearly calendar
- a page for each day's lesson planning
- space for registers
- a page to write out your timetable
- various other sections for notes, orders, etc.

Teachers use these planners in a variety of ways: some fill them out religiously in advance for each day, giving lots of detail about the lessons they will be teaching; others use them in a more haphazard style, filling them out after their lessons, perhaps as a reminder of what they have covered. It is useful to keep as much information as you possibly can in the planner, as it is then all in one place and you can carry it around easily. For instance, rather than using a mark book you could keep all your registers, seating plans and marks in the same section of the planner. In this way, after taking the register you can leave the planner open to refer to students' names, check who owes homework and so on. You could also write detentions in on the daily planning page, where you can cross them off once they have been served.

When you receive your planner, wait a short while before filling in registers, as there will often be changes to class lists at the beginning of term. Rather than writing this information out, it is easier and quicker to photocopy it to size and stick it in. Similarly, glue your school calendar on the appropriate pages rather than spending valuable time writing it out. You will, of course, experiment to find your own way of using the planner. Do remember, though, that keeping all your information in the same place will make life much easier for you.

SOME SHORT CUTS

At college you will probably have been asked to give a large amount of detail when planning. There are various reasons for this. When you first start teaching you are learning and experimenting and it is important for your tutors to see what you are doing and why. You will also have had a great deal more time when studying to spend on planning your lessons. Now, though, you have a full timetable and a large administrative workload. Should you continue to plan in such detail?

The short answer is no, but I would strongly advise you to enter enough detail in your lesson planning to allow you (or someone else) to reuse the lesson plans. If you wanted to teach the same material in a year's time, it would be a shame if you could not remember what you did (and what went well, or badly). One way to do this would be to write each lesson out in note form to keep in a file, while entering only brief notes in your planner to indicate the outline of the lesson you have done. If there are schemes of work already in existence in your school or your department, and you could use them as they are or with minor adaptations, then why not do so? There is no point in 'reinventing the wheel'. You could also ask other teachers in your department for advice on lessons that work well for them in each particular topic area.

If you are teaching the same material to more than one class, you could of course use the same lessons with each of them. A word of warning here, though: do make sure that you don't become bored and stale with your lessons. When the time comes for your lessons to be evaluated, or if inspectors arrive at your school, you will need to spend some time writing out aims and objectives for each lesson (see Chapters 15 and 16 for more information on appraisal and inspection). However, an inspection team will be more interested in seeing that departmental schemes are in place, rather than being concerned about whether you have your own detailed plans.

KNOWING YOUR SYLLABUS

To a large extent, whatever subject you are teaching, national guidelines will dictate what you have to cover in your lessons. In reality, though, you should be able to adapt your own ideas to fit in with these guidelines. Be aware of what the students (and their parents or guardians) will respond well to. For instance, there is absolutely no reason why you shouldn't teach a difficult topic that is not actually a statutory requirement for your class. Generally, students respond very well to a challenge. Their parents or guardians will also be delighted to find out that you are so keen to stretch your students.

What you teach is determined to a certain extent by your department and also by the available resources. Obviously, at General Certificate of Secondary Education (GCSE) and A level you will be teaching to a syllabus. It can sometimes be difficult to find out exactly what the syllabus requirements are, either because it is difficult for you to access a copy of the syllabus or because you find the syllabus itself hard to fathom out. It is certainly worth asking your head of department to sit down with you and explain the syllabus carefully and clearly to you. There is nothing worse than reaching the last term of a GCSE or A level course, only to find that you have not actually covered all the topics required. Long-term planning is important when teaching two-year courses, as you must be careful not to run out of time (see the section on 'Long-term planning' for some more ideas on this).

BALANCED LESSON PLANNING

Balanced lesson plans are vital for a number of reasons, but unfortunately they are quite hard to achieve. With practice, you will find that you can instinctively sense what is balanced and what is not. However, experience will only come by making mistakes in your lesson planning (and also by being willing to experiment with some more unusual ideas). Balance is essentially about lessons that utilize a variety of strategies, and which keep the students' (and the teacher's) interest. When you are trying to plan a balanced lesson, try putting yourself in the students' place (see Chapter 3) and ask yourself how you would feel if presented with the lesson and activities you have in mind. For instance, how would you react if asked to read a difficult textbook in total silence for a full hour? Wouldn't you find it much easier if, for example, you had ten minutes' reading time, and were then asked to discuss what you had discovered?

A balance of activities

This is not always possible to accomplish, for instance if you are setting a test, but as far as you can you should try to use a variety of different teaching strategies and activities in each lesson. By doing this, you will keep the students (and yourself) interested and engaged. You can also set a time limit for each task (see Chapter 3) to ensure that the students work at their maximum capacity for as long as possible. A balanced lesson will not require the students to listen to the teacher for extended periods of time, or to work in silence for more than an optimum of about 20 to 30 minutes.

There are many possibilities for different teaching strategies and activities, but I would like to offer you a few ideas and suggestions. Although traditionally associated with particular subjects, many of these ideas are applicable to a number of different areas of the curriculum. Be as 'experimental' as you like – students respond well to the unexpected. I have also provided a 'model' for a balanced lesson plan to show how you could use some of these strategies and activities.

Teaching strategies

Teacher based:
- Teacher talks to the class.
- Teacher gives instructions to the class.
- Teacher discusses a topic, getting responses from the class.
- Teacher asks the class questions.
- Teacher writes facts/figures/ideas on the board for the class to copy.
- Teacher writes the students' ideas on the board for the class to copy.

Student based:
- Students follow instructions.

- Students work in pairs or groups.
- Students make group presentations to the class.
- Students make individual presentations to the class.
- Students brainstorm for ideas.
- Students work individually, e.g. reading, writing, drawing, calculating.

Types of activities:

Reading activities:
- Individual reading.
- Reading for information.
- Memorizing facts, figures or vocabulary.
- Reading in pairs or groups.
- 'Speed' or 'skim' reading.
- Reading articles in newspapers.
- Reading from textbooks.
- Reading each other's work.

Writing activities:
- Writing essays.
- Answering questions, e.g. mathematical problems.
- Summarizing the main points of a text.
- Writing reports.
- Imaginative writing.
- Factual/analytical writing.

Drawing activities:
- Drawing diagrams.
- Drawing from life or from photographs.
- Drawing from imagination or memory.
- Creating mind maps (see Chapter 4).
- Creating brainstorms.

Speaking and listening activities:
- Discussions.
- Explanations.
- Question and answer sessions.
- Quizzes (individual or group).
- Oral presentations.
- Debates.
- Making (taping) radio programmes on a topic.
- Listening to tapes.

Physical and practical activities:
- Games and warm-ups.
- Individual skills work.
- Group exercises.
- Drawing, modelling and painting.

- Practical experiments.
- Designing, building and testing.
- Performances/demonstrations, e.g. dance, drama, science.

A model balanced lesson plan

A balanced lesson plan of one hour could contain the following strategies and activities. I have assumed an actual teaching time of 50 minutes, giving five minutes at the start of the lesson for the students to arrive and to take the register, and five minutes at the end for clearing away. Although this lesson is clearly for a writing-based subject, it could easily be adapted to fit a more practical area of the curriculum, for instance science or PE.

5 mins	Introduction to the aim and topic of the lesson by the teacher. *Teacher talks, students listen.*
10 mins	Students brainstorm ideas on the topic in their exercise books. *Students find out for themselves what they already know.*
10 mins	Ideas are correlated on the board and copied down. *This brings everyone's ideas together.*
20 mins	Students do individual writing on the topic. *Focus on individual written work for a limited time.*
5 mins	A couple of students read out their work. *Brief oral presentation to class.*

Balance for the student

In combination with balancing the different strategies and activities used, the teacher should be aware of what the students are being asked to do during a lesson. Is there too much emphasis on silent reading or writing, which requires a high level of concentration from the students? Is there a great deal of noisy activity going on which may be disruptive for the quieter students (and other classes)? Again, put yourself in your students' shoes and think about how the lesson will actually feel for them.

Occasionally, your students will want to do very little during the lesson and you should be aware of when this might happen. There is little point in forcing them to work in a particular way (e.g. writing in silence) if you are going to have to risk confrontation in order to do so, and if the work they produce is unlikely to be of any real value. For instance, a class that you see last lesson on a Friday, who have just had an hour of games on a really hot day, are highly unlikely to want to work particularly hard!

Balance for the teacher

While taking all this into account, do not forget yourself. You should ensure that there is also a balance within the lesson for you – that you are not doing all the work or all the talking. You should aim for a short period of quiet, calm individual work in each lesson if you can, so that you can have a rest from the noise created by a class of students and so that you can help individuals who may need extra attention.

From time to time, you may need a 'lesson off' and there is no need to feel at all guilty about this. For some ideas about restful lessons have a look at 'Lessons for the tired teacher' in Chapter 4. Remember, although the students may feel that they work really hard at school, it is the teacher who actually makes the majority of the effort in most situations, including controlling a group of people with a variety of different needs. So, when you need a break, give yourself one.

SHORT-TERM PLANNING

Short-term planning is daily, weekly and half-termly planning. Try to ensure that, as well as balancing each individual session, you also balance your weekly lessons so that you are not planning too many teacher-intensive sessions in one day. You should also try to set marking on a 'rota' basis, so that you cover each class adequately, and all your marking does not come at one time. This, however, is far easier to say than to do. It will help if you identify specific pieces of work or topic areas (to yourself and to the students) that you are going to spend more time on marking. It can help to draw a brief overview of your week's lessons and look at how your marking load falls. Chapter 7 gives more information on marking strategies and ways to save time.

LONG-TERM PLANNING

Long-term planning is planning for an entire term or for the whole year. Your school or head of department may well ask you to set out in advance what you intend to cover, but do remember that they will not expect you to stick rigidly to a long-term plan. There are so many variants that this type of planning is subject to, for instance, a topic may take far less time than you had anticipated or you may find that the students are particularly enjoying an area of your subject and you would like to spend more time on it.

Do try to plan the topics you have to cover in a way that gives the students some variety in their lessons. For instance, you could start by covering an area of your subject that necessitates a lot of individual work, and then follow this up with a group project. Similarly, a series of practical experiments or exercises could be followed by written review work. Again, try to take your marking load into consideration: perhaps plan to do some group discussion work just after a series of tests. In this way you will not add to those piles of unmarked books or papers sitting on your desk, awaiting your attention.

If you are teaching a two-year course, at GCSE or A level, you will need to ensure that you cover all the areas within the syllabus (see 'Knowing your syllabus' in this chapter). It is very difficult to plan realistically over two years, but I would suggest that it is better to finish early than to run out of time. If you have covered all the topics in time, then you can simply do revision work or perhaps redraft coursework.

Chapter 3

How to Control your Classes

Depending on the type of school you are teaching at, classroom control may pose little problem, or may be the most vital part of your job. However, even in the 'easiest' of schools, where the students are keen to do whatever you ask, the importance of imposing your own rules and standards should not be underestimated. In a school where the majority of students are well behaved, you may find that a relatively small number of students create problems for you. By following the suggestions in this chapter, you should be able to make even the most difficult classes respond well.

It is vital that, before you face your first class, you know the sanctions that you are going to apply for misbehaviour and also how serious you consider various types of misbehaviour to be. If you are as clear as possible about this, you can communicate your understanding to the class. On the other hand, if the students sense you are unsure about how to deal with them, they will 'try you out' and see how far they can push you.

If your school has specific policies it is best to stick to these, as the students will view you as a 'fair' teacher, who works along the same lines as other members of staff. It will be much harder for you if there is no school behaviour policy. I have given examples and suggested suitable sanctions for each level of misbehaviour. You may feel that some of these types of misbehaviour deserve stricter or softer punishments. It is really entirely a matter of personal taste and opinion.

Choose your own sanction, or find out the school policy, for each of the following misdemeanours *before* you start to teach.

Low-level misdemeanours

For example:

- minor rudeness to other students
- forgetting equipment

- not doing homework
- talking repeatedly, and so on.

The punishment for this type of misbehaviour is often a detention of ten or fifteen minutes, if possible with you and on the same day as the misdemeanour takes place. It is absolutely *vital* that you remember to enforce any detentions you set. If you don't turn up the sanction is worthless and, in fact, to do this is probably worse than imposing no sanction at all. A useful tip is to write the student's name down, in your planner if you have one, and then cross it off when the detention has been served.

Medium-level misdemeanours

For example:

- minor rudeness to the teacher
- swearing, but not *at* anyone
- chatting repeatedly and refusing to be quiet
- refusal to complete work, and so on.

I would suggest a longer detention for these types of misbehaviour, perhaps 30 minutes, sometimes called a 'departmental' or 'subject' detention. The problem with a detention of more than 20 minutes is that you must notify the parents or guardians at least a day in advance. You may well find your school has a specific way of doing this, perhaps through the student diaries. A more senior member of staff may take this type of detention.

Serious misbehaviour

For example:

- fighting
- serious swearing (*at* you)
- throwing dangerous objects, e.g. chairs
- completely ignoring the teacher's instructions, and so on.

Some schools have a backup policy for serious incidents whereby the teacher can send the student out of the room and to another member of staff. Do not become one of those teachers who sends such difficult students outside the room to stand on their own for the rest of the lesson. This is not a sanction, it is denying the student any sort of education or chance to sort out their own behaviour. You are still responsible for a student, even if they are standing outside the room, and if anything should happen to them you would be accountable.

Serious incidents like these are, thankfully, rare in most schools. They should be dealt with at a higher level, but it may well be up to you to ensure the information gets passed on. Often students who are struggling in mainstream education stay there because teachers do not *write down* details of the incidents that take place. This written evidence is essential as it will enable more senior staff to take further action. Try to write your account as soon as possible, preferably immediately after the lesson. You may feel shaken up by this type of incident and it can be useful to talk to an experienced member of staff about what happened and why.

As well as finding out the sanctions for these various types of misbehaviour, it is also essential that you find out what happens when a student fails to serve a detention or other type of punishment. Again, if a student misses a detention and you do not follow it up, you may as well have given no punishment at all. You will find that this takes quite a lot of time at first, but once the students realize that they cannot 'get away' with missing your detentions, your workload will start to lessen.

THE FIRST LESSON

Don't plan anything too ambitious for your first lesson with any class. You will spend much of the time on administrative tasks such as giving out books and on talking to them about your expectations. If you do want to do a quick exercise to see what their work is like, try to think of an original and engaging idea. For instance, if you are an English teacher, try to avoid the ubiquitous autobiographical piece where the students write about themselves and the awful 'write about what you did in the holidays'. This is fine for the students who spent the summer touring America, but demeaning and depressing for Fred who spent the whole six weeks in a caravan in Bognor with his granny.

In your first lesson you should concentrate on stamping your personality and expectations on the class. But how exactly do you do this? With experience, every teacher finds their own way, but I would like to offer two ideas for you to consider.

Seat your students alphabetically

They will moan at this one, but it is an excellent way of imposing yourself on a class right from the start. It is also a good way to learn names and you can use this as your 'excuse'. Once you have the class sitting in alphabetical order, ask for a volunteer to draw you a seating plan. You can also offer to reward the class by allowing them to move to sit where they want if their behaviour merits it. However, beware of allowing them to move too soon.

There are two ways of approaching this exercise: if there is space outside the classroom, ask the students to line up and allow them in one by one. This will take some time and you do run the risk of the students misbehaving inside or outside the classroom while they are waiting. An alternative, and probably the better option, is to draw a seating plan before the students arrive and ask them to follow it. This should avoid the stress of a chaotic start to your first lesson.

You may find that this exercise takes some time, but it is worth it. If you feel nervous about doing it in your first lesson, you could allow the students to sit where they want at first and then warn them in advance that they will be sitting alphabetically next time. The model lesson in Chapter 4 demonstrates the process of alphabetical seating.

Explain your rules clearly in the first lesson

The temptation to dive straight into your first 'real' lesson may be overwhelming, but I recommend that you spend some time (perhaps ten to fifteen minutes) discussing your ideas about classroom behaviour with your students. This way they will know that you mean business and that you have a clear idea of what your expectations are. These rules will give the students the set of boundaries that they need. Again, this idea is covered in much more detail in the next section and in the model lesson in Chapter 4.

SETTING THE BOUNDARIES

No doubt your tutors at college told you about the 'honeymoon period', the time when the students will do whatever you ask, before they have 'sussed you out'. Have no illusions about this one, it is true. For the first few lessons (if you are lucky) the students will sit and listen to you, seemingly absorbing every word you are saying. Then, just when you think it is safe to relax, they will turn into the class from hell.

So, how can you avoid this situation? Other teachers may tell you to learn from experience, that in a few years' time you will find it easy to control your classes. This, however, is not much use when you are starting out as a teacher. The last thing you want is to spend a whole year suffering before you get a chance to make a fresh start with a new set of classes. And believe me, once you have 'lost' a class, it is extremely difficult to get them back.

What the students really need at the start of your time teaching them is for you to set the boundaries for them. If you do this effectively, and *stick to it*, you will make life much easier for yourself. You will learn with experience exactly what boundaries you want to set for your students, but the list in Table 3.1 may be of use for the time being.

Table 3.1 *Boundaries for students*

Boundary	Reason/reward	Sanction
No one talks when I am.	We can get on with the lesson. It's rude – I listen to you.	2 warnings, then a detention.
You arrive on time to lessons.	Lateness is rude. Interruptions are frustrating.	A detention 2x amount late by or 2x lates = a detention.
Use appropriate language.	It shows respect.	Immediate detention.
Always try your hardest.	I want you to succeed.	2 warnings, then a detention.
Do your homework (properly).	You will improve faster.	Detention to complete it.
Sometimes we work in silence.	We can all concentrate. 5 minute 'time-outs' to talk.	2 warnings, then a detention.
Show respect for others.	They will reciprocate.	2 warnings, then a detention.
Do not call out – hands up.	We can hear the answer.	Ignore those who call out.
Work as neatly as you can.	I can see to mark it.	Redo work neatly at home.
Bring the correct equipment.	We can get on with the lesson.	Instant detention. (This is harsh, but they won't forget again.)

TEN TRIED AND TESTED TEACHING TIPS

Teachers are constantly bombarded with information and advice, and it can all seem a bit overwhelming at times. This, of course, is exactly what reading a book is all about, so at this point I would like to offer ten straightforward tips for you to refer to at moments of crisis or despair:

Ten Tried and Tested Teaching Tips

1. Wait for them.

2. Perfect the deadly stare.

3. Strike a balance.

4. Put yourself in their shoes.

5. Avoid confrontation
(also known as 'you get what you deserve').

6. Praise one, encourage all.

7. Quiet teachers get quiet classes.

8. Explain, repeat, explain.

9. Always set a time limit.

10. Give one instruction at a time.

Wait for them

If there was only one piece of advice I could give teachers about classroom management, it would be this: wait for them. If you do this from the very start, they will know that it is the way you work. Do not open your mouth until you have *complete* silence, and I mean complete. Do not start talking until every single student is looking directly at you. Even if you have to stand with your arms folded for 5 minutes, eventually they will come to you. If you fight for them now, it will only get worse.

This idea is so useful and important that I am going to repeat it again. *Do not open your mouth until you have complete and total silence and every student is sitting still and looking at you.* Fold your arms, look impatient, check your watch, take out the novel you are in the middle of reading, do some knitting, gaze at the view out of the window, but on no account talk to a class of students who are not listening. This one action will stamp a considerable amount of authority on you for absolutely no effort.

It can seem scary at first, but I promise you if you wait they will come to you, especially in your very first lesson. If you start to panic try using tips (2) and (6) – the deadly stare and praise one, encourage all. If you still cannot achieve silence, keep your mouth closed and go and stand right beside any student who is still talking. Invade their personal space and they will quickly become quiet.

Perfect the deadly stare

As a teacher, you have access to many different forms of communication, perhaps the most effective of which is the 'deadly stare'. Perfect this and you will never have to ask for silence again. You will be able to walk into a classroom and stare your students into submission. There is no easy way of describing the 'deadly stare', but you will know when you have perfected it. The 'deadly stare' says: *'I am the teacher, I am in charge, and if you do not close your mouth, stop talking and wait for my commands, you are likely to suffer in the most horrible way known to humankind. So, be sensible, be quiet and let's get on with the lesson.'* And all that without opening your mouth!

Strike a balance

Teaching is about balance in so many ways, but unfortunately this is one of the hardest things to actually achieve. You need to develop a sense of 'where the students are coming from'. By this I mean they will react well to a teacher who moulds their teaching style to suit the class. With time, you will use a very different attitude and style with a class of 15-year-olds and with one of 11-year-olds. You will only be storing up trouble for yourself if what you demand does not match the capabilities and expectations of the class.

For instance, a 'bottom' set in an examination year may well be disillusioned with school. If they feel they are not going to do particularly well in their exams, they will resent a teacher who tries to force them to work hard all the time. Far better to reason and negotiate with them. Try asking them to work solidly for 20 minutes, then have a 5 minute break for a chat. The younger the students are, the more willing they will be to do exactly what you say (usually). Top sets will probably respond well if you challenge them academically. In fact, this is actually true of any class. The vast majority of students respond very well to ideas that you may feel are beyond their capacity. Try them out and surprise yourself (and them).

Put yourself in their shoes

This is worth doing whenever something or someone is frustrating you. That brilliant lesson you spent three hours planning is going wrong? Put yourself in your students' shoes and try to see it from their point of view – what would they feel is wrong with it? The students at the back of the class keep talking and passing love notes while you are trying to explain the finer points of quadratic equations. Put yourself in their shoes – you were young once, sometimes school can be just plain boring, no matter how good the teacher is.

Avoid confrontation (also known as 'you get what you deserve')

If someone is screaming at you, how does it make you feel? Now think about how a young student must feel if a teacher shouts at them. You would not behave like this if you worked in an office, would you, so why do it to your students? If you do choose to shout at them, be aware that they will probably shout back at you. In teaching, you get what you deserve, and if you do not show respect for your students, it is far more likely that confrontations will occur.

Confrontations can arise for many reasons in the classroom. You are human, and sometimes controlling 30 students can be exhausting. Do try, though, to keep yourself calm at all times. You will get far better results by reasoning with someone rather than confronting them. Occasionally a student will become confrontational with you, apparently for no good reason. If this happens, try to point out quietly and reasonably why their behaviour is unacceptable, avoiding (if you can) rising to their bait.

Praise one, encourage all

You were no doubt told at college that praise is a very effective teaching tool. However, generalized praise (although useful) has its limits. Next time you want a class to behave in a certain way, try singling out one individual who is already doing what you want. *'That's great, Sundip, it looks like you're ready to get on with the lesson, because you're sitting really quietly and waiting for me to take the register. Well done.'* This is far more effective than moaning at the class to be quiet. This is also a good backup tip for when 'Wait for them' and 'The deadly stare' are not working.

Quiet teachers get quiet classes

On one teaching practice I worked with a class that had two teachers, one for Monday to Wednesday and one for Thursday and Friday. They were both excellent teachers, but one spoke really quietly to the class and the other was much louder. The difference in the classroom noise levels amazed me – with the quiet teacher, the students had to listen far more carefully, and so the class was quieter as a whole.

Take a moment, when you are teaching, to listen to yourself. How loud are you? And just how loud do you really need to be? Think of the image of turning the volume down on a stereo and try to do the same with your voice. Obviously, you need to be careful not to take this to extremes. I have encountered teachers who speak so quietly that no one can actually hear them!

Explain, repeat, explain

One of the biggest problems inexperienced teachers face is the frustrations caused by misunderstandings in the classroom. You know the scenario from teaching practice: you spend five minutes explaining to the class what you want them to do, they start to work, then a few seconds later three hands go up – 'Miss/Sir, I don't understand . . . what did you say I have to do?'

Remember, the students are being bombarded with new information, particularly at the start of term and particularly those new to a school. This is where the strategy of 'explain, repeat, explain' comes in.

1. *Explain*   Tell the class what you want them to do.
2. *Repeat*   Choose a student (perhaps one who looks as if they are not listening) and ask them to repeat what you just said. If they cannot, ask for someone who can to raise a hand. By hearing the students' interpretation of what you said, you may find out that they did not understand the instructions you gave.
3. *Explain*   Repeat the instructions again in your own words, clarifying any areas of uncertainty, and then ask: *'Is there anyone who's not sure what we're going to do?'*

This might sound patronizing, but it really does help clarify any misunderstandings and also encourages the students to listen carefully the first time. There may also be genuine misunderstandings taking place, perhaps because you are not experienced in giving clear instructions, or the students are not yet used to your way of working.

Always set a time limit

As I have mentioned before, your students *want* boundaries. They are still unsure of where they stand in the world and what is expected of them. Even as adults we crave the security of knowing what we are expected to do. Why then, do teachers set a task without letting their students know how long they have to complete it? Always let them know, whether it is three minutes, twenty minutes or five lessons. Think about how human beings work – we are always more efficient when we have a deadline, for instance in an exam.

Once you have set your time limit and allowed the students to start working on the task, give them a constant reminder of how long they have left. Your time limit can be flexible, according to how quickly you think the students are progressing, or you could say to them, *'When you see that it's ten past ten, I'd like you all to stop working and wait for the next instruction. I'm not going to remind you about the time, I'd like to see how well you can observe this time limit yourselves.'* When the deadline arrives, some of the more observant students will notice and stop working. As the noise levels drop, the others will (hopefully) begin to understand what is happening.

Give one instruction at a time

It is very tempting to give a class a long list of instructions to follow, particularly if you are setting a complicated task, but it is actually very hard for students (and adults) to take in a lot of information at once. It is far better to give one instruction at a time, stopping between each to ensure that the students have understood what you want them to do. Again, this will avoid problems with misunderstandings and students continually asking what they have to do.

LEARNING NAMES

There is no overestimating how difficult learning names can be. This is particularly true for teachers of subjects such as PE and music, who may have a large number of classes, some of which they only see for an hour a week. There are a variety of strategies that you could use in order to help you learn your students' names, and I would strongly recommend that you put them into use immediately you start with any class. One of the simplest strategies is to use their names as often as possible, whenever you address them.

Until you have a good idea of the students' names, it is very hard to control them effectively. A reprimand is always much more powerful if you can use the student's name; similarly praise is far better if you can personalize it. You will probably find it fairly easy to learn the names of the 'good' students, who always answer questions, and the 'bad' students, who are always messing around. However, when it comes to writing reports, it can be extremely embarrassing if you cannot remember which student fits which name (or even which gender they are). Here are a few ideas that have worked for me.

Name games

If you teach a subject such as drama, you will probably know quite a few name games already, which involve the students moving around in an open space. Unfortunately, for the majority of subjects, the students will have to stay in their seats. Here are some adaptations of drama games that you can use in a static position. These 'games' are probably best suited to your younger students:

- *The adjective game*   The students find an adjective to describe themselves, starting with the same letter as their name, e.g. 'My name is Sue and I am stupendous.'
- *Pass the name*   To start, the student says their own name, and then the name of the person they are passing to. Anyone who pauses or makes a mistake is out. 'Tim to Anna, Anna to Chirag, Chirag to Shami', and so on. Ask the students to pass to someone of the opposite sex, to make it harder and to avoid friends passing to friends all the time.
- *Pass the name (version 2)*   This is a combination of the two games above and requires the students to remember each other's adjectives: 'Terrible Tim to Anxious Anna, Anxious Anna to Careful Chirag, Careful Chirag to Silly Shami', and so on.

Use a seating plan

Once you have your students settled in their places, ask one of them to draw you a seating plan. Not only will this save you time and effort, but they will probably know each other's names better than you do. Refer to this seating plan (which should preferably be on the same page as your register – see 'The teacher's planner' in Chapter 2) as often as possible. Whenever you ask a question of a specific student, always use their name.

Make notes on your register

This can be a useful way of identifying easily recognizable students, or of telling two students with the same name apart. For instance if you have two 'Emmas' in your class, but one wears glasses, you can easily write this beside the name. A word of warning here: sometimes your students will ask if they can call out the register. This happened to me once, and it was only half-way through that I realized I had written some rather cutting comments beside the names!

Memory systems

Memory systems can seem rather silly when you have never used them before but, believe me, they work. There are various books on the subject that you could study if you want to find out more. At the most basic level memory systems require you to make links in your mind. The links you are looking for are ones that are easily memorable. For some reason the human brain seems to work better if the connections are weird or unusual.

Probably the best way to explain this is to give a few examples. To save the blushes of my former students, I have made up the names and links. Say you have a student called Jane, who is very intelligent, but whose name you keep forgetting. Try thinking to yourself, 'Jane has a big brain.' I know it sounds stupid, but the fact that this rhymes will make it more memorable. To make the link visual as well, you could imagine Jane having an enormous head to contain her big brain. Similarly, if you had a student called Mona who was always complaining, you could remember 'moany Mona' and so on. Physical characteristics can also give you useful memory hooks.

The gentle art of bluff

Sometimes, despite all your attempts, there are students whose names you cannot remember. The week of reports comes and you are panicking. You only have one more lesson with these students before you have to comment on them. What can you do? Here are a few strategies that I am not ashamed to say I have used, involving the 'gentle art of bluff'.

- *Question and answer*   Ask a question using the name of a specific student and then look to see who answers.
- *State your name*   Set a group or individual task and ask the students to state their names before they start their presentation.
- *Off you go*   Ask the students to stand behind their chairs or get ready to leave by name order. When you call out the names of the students you do not know, look to see who moves.
- *Ask for help*   Ask a student you can trust to be discreet for the name that you cannot remember. They will be delighted that you have asked for their assistance. It is worth showing that you need help too (but only occasionally).
- *Name your reward*   Give out merit marks (or whatever rewards your school uses) and as you write them into the student's diary, check their name.

DEVELOPING A STYLE OF YOUR OWN

As you look around your school and hear the students talking about other members of staff, you will start to see how teachers each have their own individual style. This is entirely a matter of taste, and of course depends a great deal on the class you are teaching, but in my experience I have found that some approaches are far more effective than others. It is worth considering the impact of the following aspects of your style on your students.

What you wear

This will vary according to the subject you teach and the type of school you teach in. For instance, if you are a PE or drama teacher, you may need to wear loose clothing so that you can demonstrate activities for the students. If your school has a strict uniform code for the students, it is likely that the head expects the teachers to dress smartly as well. If you are inexperienced, I would advise against wearing clothing that is too casual. If you dress smartly you will give your students the impression that you 'mean business'.

What you say

The phrases you use and the way you speak will all communicate a certain style to the students. You will probably find that you talk to them in a very different way to the way that you talk to your friends and other adults. We all adapt the way we speak according to the situations we are in and the impression we want to give, so be aware of this, particularly in your early lessons.

How you maintain order

The way you create discipline (or fail to) will give out strong messages about your style as a teacher. The ideal situation is for the students to view you as firm but fair. You should apply exactly the same rules for every student, but do be aware that certain situations and individuals will call for careful handling (see 'Setting the Boundaries' and 'Strike a balance' in this chapter).

How you set and mark work

Again, this will have an impact on how the students view you. If your lessons are interesting, well structured and have clear aims (see Chapter 4), you will maintain your students' interest. If you set lots of work that you ask the students to complete quickly, but fail to mark, they will feel that you are being unreasonable. On the other hand, if you never set homework and allow the students to work at their own pace, they may well like you, but whether they will respect you is another matter.

What you do

Teachers should be careful to avoid saying one thing and doing another. If you expect your students to behave well, but you treat them without respect, you are storing up trouble for yourself. If you set the boundaries at the start and stick to them in a fair manner, the students will know exactly where they stand. It is important for you to have interests outside school as well. Your students want to feel that you are human and that you take an interest in wider issues, including the latest cultural developments. If you can comment on matters of interest to them, or even incorporate them into your lessons, they are much more likely to respond positively to you.

How you set up your classroom

If you are lucky, you may have a space of your own, a classroom that you teach in all the time. Be aware that the students will make judgements about you by looking at your room. Setting out a classroom in rows gives a very different message to grouping the tables. This is, of course, a matter of personal opinion as well as being dictated by the type of room you have. See the following section for more comments on this.

How well you relate to the students

Although you want your students to view you as a firm, even a strict teacher, this does not mean that you cannot relate to them. They will work better for you if they feel that you have an interest in them and that you care about how well they do at school. Relating to the students should not, however, be translated as relaxing with them.

MANAGING THE SPACE

The way you set up your classroom will send out strong messages about you and will also have an impact on the way that you teach. It is worth thinking carefully about how practical each layout is before you start. There is no reason why you should not start with the desks in rows and then change the layout later in the term. There is also no reason why you should not move furniture for specific lessons, but do bear in mind that there are administrative problems associated with this that you must deal with. If you are using someone else's classroom, you will make yourself extremely unpopular if you move the furniture, but do not return it to its previous position.

Desks in rows

- *Advantages*   All the students will be facing the front. This makes it easier to check that they are listening and also enables them all to see the board easily. You can give out and collect in resources and books along each row, to make life easier. The students will view you as a 'traditional' teacher (not necessarily an advantage).
- *Disadvantages*   It is difficult to do any meaningful group or discussion work without substantial rearrangement of the furniture. There may be the temptation to ignore

the ends of rows, where you cannot see the students so easily. You will only be able to give individual help to two students at a time. This style of layout does tend to encourage 'chalk and talk' teaching, i.e. the teacher standing at the front, talking to the class and writing notes on the board.

Desks in groups

- *Advantages* Group work and discussions can take place easily. You can also talk to a whole group of students at a time. You are forced to move around the classroom more and so this encourages an interactive style of teaching.
- *Disadvantages* The students may not be able to see the board so easily. It is harder to ensure that all students are looking at you and not talking if some of them have their backs to you. It might prove harder to give out resources.

CREATING GROUPS

For some activities you will need the students to work in groups, and creating these groups can be a challenge in itself. I would advise against planning group work when you are new to your classes, so that when you do attempt it the students have a very clear idea about your expectations of their behaviour. In this way, you are less likely to encounter problems. Before starting on any group work, there are various considerations for you to think about.

Moving the furniture

If you have chosen to arrange your desks in rows, make sure that you allow sufficient time for moving the furniture and returning it to its former position. Rather than having a free-for-all, it is worth taking some time over this and asking one group of students at a time to rearrange their desks. You will also need to decide the best layout of desks for the type of work you want to do.

Combinations

Keep a careful eye on the combinations in each group. You will need to ensure that any troublemakers are kept separate, as they have a tendency to gravitate together. You will also need to ensure that there is a good mix in each group, with leaders as well as followers, although do be wary of putting too many strong personalities together.

How to group

Before you go ahead with any group work, decide whether you are going to create the groups yourself, or whether you are going to allow the students to do so. If you are only doing the occasional bit of group work, there is probably no harm in allowing them to decide groupings for themselves. However, if group work plays an essential part in your subject (for instance drama or PE) you will need to set the groups yourself to ensure that the students work with a variety of others, rather than just with their friends. This will also avoid the situation where one (unpopular) student is 'left out' of the groupings.

   If the group work is going to go on for a while, you should probably spend some time working them out in advance, so that you get a good mix in each. An excellent way of creating 'instant' mixed groups is by numbering the students. For instance, if you want groups of three and you have 30 students in your class, ask them to count around the room up to ten. All the ones will then work together, all the twos and so on. This works for groups of any size.

Chapter 4

How to Teach your Classes

THE IMPORTANCE OF AIMS

I can remember very clearly my lecturers at college going on and on about aims, but they never made any sense to me until I actually started teaching. The importance of having an aim goes back to the idea of the students needing boundaries: they need boundaries so that they know how you want them to behave and, similarly, they need boundaries so that they know what you want them to learn. By setting an aim for each lesson, the teacher is simply giving the students information about what they want the class to achieve during that period of time. By explaining the aim the teacher demonstrates to the students the purpose of the work they are doing. This equates to the discussion about why we need classroom rules, in Chapter 3.

You should state your aim at the very beginning of each lesson: this is what we are going to aim to achieve today. This will give the students a target to aim at, just as setting a time limit for any piece of work does (again, see Chapter 3). You should then keep referring back to your aim during the lesson to keep the students on task and on target. Finally, you should use the aim to summarize the lesson right at the end – have we achieved what we set out to do? If we have, then we know we have learnt something – and praise is in order.

This stating and restating of your aim may seem rather pedantic – the sort of thing your lecturers asked you to do at college, that you could never see a reason for. Once again, though, put yourself in your students' shoes. If a teacher just launches into a subject, without explaining what is happening or where the lesson is going, they will feel 'at sea' and unsure about what you require of them or what you want them to learn. The intrinsic human tendency to place an order or structure on our experiences means that, without realizing it, they will piece together exactly what the aim is for themselves. To avoid confusion, and to save time and effort, the teacher should do this for his or her students.

A MODEL FIRST LESSON

At this point, rather than giving you more tips or rules about how to behave with, and teach, your classes, I would like to offer a model for a first lesson to give you something concrete to 'hang on to'. This is not model in the sense of a perfect lesson, but it does give a suggested structure for you to follow. It is intended as a guide only and is based on a first-year secondary school class doing a subject where written work is used, for example English or history. However, many of the points made and strategies adopted here will apply to students of different ages and in different subjects. As explained in Chapter 3, the majority of this first lesson with a class will be spent on explaining your rules and expectations.

The model is set out like a play script: I have included details of what the teacher does and says, a commentary that explains the reasons behind her comments and actions, and also some possible student reactions (and why the students might react in this way). I have assumed a lesson length of about an hour.

(*The students arrive in dribs and drabs as they have had trouble finding the classroom.*)

> COMMENT: The teacher does not feel this slight lateness is a problem in the first lesson with first years and does not make an issue of it. This may be different with a class of older students who should know their way around.

(*As they arrive the teacher directs them towards the seating plan she has made and put up on the wall. They are to sit in alphabetical order.*)

Teacher: (*to individuals and small groups of students*) Have a look at this seating plan I've made and see how quickly you can find your place. Well done, Ahmed, that was really quick.

> COMMENT: The teacher has challenged them to make the seating plan seem like a competition rather than a control mechanism. She has then praised an individual student by name (she knows his name from the position he is sitting in) to encourage the others.

Teacher: While you're waiting for everyone to arrive, you can chat quietly among yourselves.

> COMMENT: The teacher knows that there is no chance or point in getting them silent and then being constantly interrupted. Far better to make them feel you have been generous enough to 'allow' them to talk for a while.

(*After a few minutes the students have all arrived and are seated alphabetically. The teacher has a copy of the seating plan in her planner, alongside the register. She now folds her arms and waits for them to notice that she is ready to start. They gradually become silent.*)

Teacher: Right, before I start I'd like to make sure that *everyone* is sitting still and looking directly at me. (*she waits a moment*) As you know from your timetables, my name is Miss Cowley and I'm going to be your teacher this year. You can see how to spell my name, because I've written it on the noticeboard over there. (*She indicates the board and the students look.*) Now, in today's lesson we are going to aim to get through lots of administrative tasks: checking names, discussing our rules, giving out books and so on.

> COMMENT: The teacher has waited for the complete attention of all the students. She has informed the class what the aim for this lesson is and why. She will refer back to her aim later, to ensure that it remains explicit.

Teacher: The first thing I'd like to do is to take the register, so that I can check that everyone is here and learn how to pronounce your names. I'll also be able to check that you're sitting alphabetically, as on my seating plan. If I do pronounce them incorrectly please let me know.

Student: (*nervously calling out*) Miss, miss, I didn't realize we had to sit where you said. I'm in the wrong place. (*Other students start to call out that they're in the wrong places too.*)

> COMMENT: The teacher should have stated 'Put your hands up if you think you're in the wrong place.' She has also given rather a lot of information at once and this may confuse them (see Chapter 3 'Give one instruction at a time').

Teacher: (*waits for silence with arms folded*) Please put your hand up if you think you might be sitting in the wrong place. (*Thankfully only four hands go up.*) Now, one at a time please go and check on the seating plan where you should be sitting. You first. (*They do so and swop themselves around.*) Now, let's get on with the register. Ahmed.

(*As the teacher calls out each name she looks up to see the student to check that she is pronouncing it correctly.*)

Teacher: Okay, well done. That's how I will start every lesson, by taking the register, so that I can find out who is here and also check if anybody arrives late. As you can see, I have a lot of names to learn and I'm going to need your help to do it over the next few weeks. You might be wondering why you're sitting in alphabetical order, well that's why, so that I can learn your names. Once I have learnt them, and I'm sure you are behaving yourselves very well, I might allow you to move next to your friends.

> COMMENT: The teacher has started to develop the idea of a partnership – they will have to help her learn their names. She has also explained why they are sitting like this, to pre-empt the question that would no doubt have cropped up soon. She has also made it clear when and how she will allow them to move to sit somewhere else.

Teacher: The first thing I'd like to do today is to explain exactly what I expect of you in my lessons. That way you'll be clear about what you have to do and about what you shouldn't do. If you have any questions at any time, please raise your hands rather than calling out, so that I can hear what each of you has to say. I'm afraid that you will have to sit still and listen for a while, but I'll try to be as brief as I can.

> COMMENT: The teacher is now going to explain her boundaries to the class and she has referred back to the aim of the lesson. She has reiterated the point about raising hands to ask questions and has also explained why this is necessary. She has warned them in advance that they are going to have to listen carefully for a while.

Teacher: The first and most important rule in my lessons is that nobody talks while somebody else is, particularly while I am. Can anybody tell me why this is so important?

Student: I can, Miss!

Teacher: (*Ignores the student who has called out and checks seating plan for the name of a student who has his/her hand up.*) Yasmin, you've remembered to put your hand up, well done. Can you tell me why this is so important?

Yasmin: So that we can hear what you are saying, Miss.

Teacher: That's right. Very good. It's very important that everyone can hear what I am saying. You will also need to listen to each other very carefully. Now, what do you think the punishment will be if you do talk while I am talking Yasmin?

Yasmin: A detention, Miss?

Teacher: That's right, but to show how fair and reasonable I am I will give you two warnings first. After that, if you talk again I will give you a 15-minute, same day detention which I will take. If you still keep talking the detention will go up to 30 minutes. If you find it impossible to stay quiet, I'm afraid I will have no alternative but to send you to ... (the head of department).

> COMMENT: By ignoring the student who has called out, the teacher has made it clear by her behaviour that she does not want them to do this, without having to state it explicitly. After the student has answered correctly she has used praise and then repeated the rule, developing the answer a little (see Chapter 3 'Explain, repeat, explain'). She has then gone on to make the sanction for this misbehaviour clear. The sanctions stated will obviously depend on the individual teacher or school.

Teacher: Now, my second rule is that you all arrive on time to lessons, so that we can start work immediately. Put your hand up if you can tell me what you think you should do if another teacher keeps you behind, or if there is any other reason that you are late. Yes, Ben, what do you think?

Ben: We should get them to write a note in our diary, Miss?

Teacher: That's right again. Well done. And if you come to a lesson late without a very good reason, I'm afraid I shall have to keep you behind after school to make up the time. Now let's talk about how we should approach our work. Does anyone have any ideas about this? Put your hands up if you do.

COMMENT: Although it appears that the rules are now being opened for discussion, it is fairly straightforward to elicit the responses you want or to mould the students' replies to suit you. The teacher will continue to go through all her boundaries in this way (see Chapter 3) until the class have understood. It may be useful to write them down on the board as you do so. This 'setting boundaries' could take about 10 to 20 minutes, but it is worth while.

Teacher: Now that we've gone through the behaviour I expect in my lessons, I'd like to give out the exercise books. When you get your book I want you to write the following information on the front cover as neatly as you can. (*She writes this information on the board for them to copy: the subject; her name; the student's name and class.*) When you've finished doing that, I'd like you to sit quietly and wait for the next instruction. Any questions? No? Okay, who would like to volunteer to give out some books? Danny has his hand up and is sitting quietly, so does Claire.

COMMENT: The teacher has given clear instructions to the students and ensured that they get this right by using the board. She has also told them what they should do when they have finished – the students will complete this task at different rates. She has chosen to 'reward' the two students who are following her instructions by asking them to give out the books.

(*They give the books out. While the students are filling in the front cover the teacher walks around and checks that they are doing it correctly.*)

Teacher: Now, before we start writing in our new books, I'd like to talk to you about how you should set out your work in them and how you should treat them. I'd like us to find about five rules to go in the very front. Can anyone put their hand up with an idea? Yes, Chirag?

Chirag: We should write as neatly as we can, Miss.

Teacher: Very good, Chirag. Jenny, can you tell me why you think this is important?

Jenny: So that you can read it, Miss?

Teacher: That's right. It's very important that I can read your work, so that I can mark it. Before we put that rule in, though, there's something that we're going to need at the top of the page. Who can suggest what it is?

COMMENT: The student has indeed offered one of the rules the teacher wants, but before they write down this particular rule she wants them to say that they should always put a title and date at the top of their work. This needs to come first, as they are going to need a title for their list of rules. She has asked a leading question to get the response she wants. She can then write the title and date on the board and the first rule which will be 'Always put a title and the date on your work.' After this she can go back to Chirag's idea and any other rules she wants. It is worth putting rules about how to work at the front of an exercise book, so that they can be easily referred to if the students are not following them.

(*Once the rules have been 'negotiated' and written up on the board, the students copy them down while the teacher moves around the classroom and checks how they are doing. After a while, some finish their work and want to know what to do next.*)

> COMMENT: The teacher did not let the class know what to do after they had finished. There are two options now: she could stop the whole class and let them know what the next task is, or she could let these few individuals talk for a few moments until the majority have finished.

(*After a few minutes it is clear that most of the students have finished.*)

Teacher: Okay, I think nearly all of you have finished now, so I'd like everyone to look this way so that I can explain what I want you to do next. Anyone who hasn't finished can then go back to copying the rules down. (*She waits until she has everyone's attention.*) Now, I'm going to set you an exercise so that I can see what you are good at and what you need help with. Put your hand up if you can remember the rule I told you about what we do when we are working individually. Yes, Rizwan.

Rizwan: We work quietly, Miss?

Teacher: That's very good. You work in complete silence so that we can all concentrate.

(*The teacher now goes through the task she wants the class to complete, writing a title and the date on the board and questioning them to make sure they have understood.*)

Teacher: Right, if you look at the clock you will see that we only have 15 minutes until the end of the lesson. I'm going to give you 10 minutes to complete this task, so that we have time to clear up at the end of the lesson. Are there any questions? No? Off you go then.

(*The students start to work, but one of them, Emily, starts to chat to her next door neighbour.*)

Teacher: Emily, do you have a question that you'd like to ask me?

> COMMENT: Roughly translated as 'I've checked whether the class had any questions and they didn't, I've told you we're not going to talk while working, so why on earth have you started chatting?' Combined with the 'deadly stare' this will hopefully persuade Emily to be quiet.

(*Emily becomes quiet, but a few minutes later she starts to talk again.*)

Teacher: Emily, I have made it perfectly clear that you are not to talk while you are working, so I am now giving you your first warning. Do you understand?

Emily: Yes, Miss.

(*Emily becomes quiet again, but a few minutes later she starts chatting again to her friend, Jessica, who talks back to her.*)

Teacher: Jessica, I can see that you've decided to talk as well, so I'm going to give you your first warning. Can you tell me what will happen after your second warning?

Jessica: A detention, Miss?

Teacher: That's right. And it would be a real shame to get a detention in your very first lesson with me, wouldn't it? Now can you get on with your work in silence please and stop disturbing the class. We have five minutes left, everybody.

> COMMENT: It is sometimes better to pick on the person who is being chatted to, rather than the one who is talking. This works because there is no point in someone talking if they are getting no response. The teacher has used this strategy and has made the sanction for ignoring her instructions very clear. It would be a shame to have to give out detentions in the very first lesson, but as it is almost time to finish, she will probably not have to do this. She has reminded the class about how much time they have left and will do so again as the time runs out.

(*A few minutes later.*)

Teacher: You have one minute left now, so I'd like you to try and finish off the section that you are doing. When you have finished, please close your book and make a pile in the centre of your tables. (*A minute later.*) Okay, time's up, please stop and put your books in the middle of the table. Can I have two volunteers to collect the books in please? (*Lots of hands go up and the teacher chooses two students.*)

(*When the books have been collected in, the teacher stands with her arms folded and waits for silence. She has overrun a little and the buzzer for break goes, but she does not move. Eventually the students become silent, the more observant ones 'shushing' the others.*)

> COMMENT: It is really important to have an orderly end to the lesson, as it ensures the students go away in a calm frame of mind. They will hopefully remember your excellent classroom control for the next lesson. The teacher is fortunate that it is break next, as the students are keen to go out to play. If it was not, she would have problems because she would be making them late for their next lesson. It is much better to end too early, rather than too late. You can always 'string out' the standing behind chairs exercise (see Chapter 1) by allowing one group at a time to push their chairs in and then 'practise' standing in silence.

Teacher: Right, as you can hear, the buzzer for break has gone, but I have a couple of things to say to you before we go, so can I have everyone looking at me? (*She waits a moment.*) Now, first of all I'd like to say that you've behaved yourselves well this lesson and we've got through all those administrative tasks that I wanted to complete – well done. However, next time I see you I want you to sit in alphabetical order again so that I can carry on learning your names. Secondly, at the end of every lesson with me I will ask you to stand behind your chairs. When everyone is standing still and silent behind their chairs I will dismiss you one group at a time. (*Some of the students go to stand behind their chairs.*) I don't believe I heard anyone say 'stand behind your chairs' did I? Please sit back down. (*She waits for them to do so.*) Okay, please stand quietly behind your chairs.

(*When they are all standing silent and ready she dismisses them, one group at a time, choosing the best behaved and quietest group first.*)

COMMENT: The teacher has praised the class to reinforce the behaviour they have learned. She has also restated the aim of the lesson so that the students understand what they have achieved. It may seem petty to make them sit back down, but it shows the class that they must wait for the teacher's command. By dismissing the best-behaved group first, she is making a point about who will receive the rewards in her lessons.

LESSONS FOR THE TIRED TEACHER

In the first term of the school year, you will probably be full of enthusiasm and energy, rising happily to the challenge of any problems that crop up. However, towards the end of this term (or possibly half-term) you may well find yourself becoming tired, both physically and emotionally. Later in this chapter you will find more details about taking care of yourself and avoiding tiredness, but at this point I would like to offer a few suggestions for lessons you can use to add some variety to your teaching and perhaps give yourself a bit of a rest.

The important idea to grasp hold of is that it is the students who should be doing the work, rather than you. Individual work tends to be less teacher-intensive than group work, where you will have the problem of noise levels to contend with (a lot of noise can be tiring in itself). However, this is not always the case, for instance, in 'Show and tell' below. These suggestions are not subject specific and you should be able to adapt them easily to your own area of specialization.

Look it up

Give each student a dictionary or a textbook. Make this a competition to encourage an enthusiastic response. The students must look up the words or subjects that you give them as quickly as they can. When they find the relevant page, they should raise their hand. They then read out the meaning or passage to the rest of the class. If you have the energy, you can reward them. You can extend this exercise by asking them to write down the definitions or passages into their exercise books. This will make the task a longer one and give you more of a rest.

Time for a test

Tests are always a good backup for when you are exhausted. The class will have to work in silence, preferably for a whole lesson. The only drawback with this is the marking involved, but you can adopt one of the strategies listed in Chapter 7 to save yourself time.

Time for the television

I would guard against the temptation to show endless videos to your classes, but there are certainly occasions when this is educationally justified and it is definitely a good way of having a 'lesson off'. If you are lucky, you may find a long video that takes more than one lesson to show. Ensure that the video links with the work you have been doing and make sure you book it in advance. There is nothing worse than planning a television lesson and then finding out that the television and video are already in use. If you can, it is worth setting up the equipment before your students arrive, so that you are fully prepared. This will also guard against the equally dreadful eventuality of the video not working.

Private reading

This works well with a class of young students but can also be successful with well-motivated older students. Basically, it involves them sitting in silence reading a book. You could even plan this for a specific lesson each week, perhaps on a Friday when you (and they) will be tired. The students could bring in their own books related to the subject you are studying. Make sure that you have backup copies as some students may forget to bring their own books, or may not have access to them.

A library visit

If you are lucky enough to have a good library in your school, and a helpful librarian, you could plan some library visits for your students where you ask them to look up information relating to their work, for instance for a project. One of the basic rules of a library is that the students should be silent, so this can be very restful for the tired teacher, who will be acting as a supervisor.

Computers

Again, if you are lucky, you may have a suite of computers in your school that you can book. The first few lessons in a computer room will be stressful, particularly if you have to induct the students yourself. However, once the students are confident about using the computers they will settle quickly to work and will quite happily stare silently at the computer screens. You can use the chance to visit a computer room as a reward, or build it into a scheme of work, so that you visit on a regular basis, perhaps even once a week.

Remember that there is a wide range of work, not just word processing, that can be accomplished on computers. For instance, a maths teacher could show his or her students how to set up a database; an art teacher could do graphics and design work; and a geography teacher could do map-based exercises. If you are very lucky, your school may be linked to the Internet, and this opens up to your students material on a huge variety of subjects.

Project work

A project on a specific area of your subject will take a long time to complete and will require the students to work in an independent way. You could allow them to choose their own subject for the project, or you could provide a list of tasks that they must complete. This works best with a well-motivated class, who are able to work on their own. A project can prove more stressful than it is worth if you have a class who will be constantly going off task. You could combine this project work with visits to the library and the computer room.

Show and tell

Although this is generally regarded as a drama activity, it can be adapted to most subjects. The students spend part of the lesson time preparing a presentation or performance that they then show to the rest of the class. This keeps your involvement to a minimum, but you will have the opportunity to mark their work during the lesson (see Chapter 7).

TEACHING SKILLS

There seems to be such a strong emphasis in schools on teaching *subjects*, that we forget, or do not have time, to teach the students the *skills* that they need to succeed. For instance, in a two-year GCSE course, a great deal of time is spent covering the syllabus, but very little thought seems to go into teaching the students revision skills or, indeed, how to take exams. The more able students manage to get by, perhaps because they work out how to structure their studying without even realizing it, but I do believe that we fail the less able students if we do not teach them at least the basic study skills.

You may feel that you have little enough time as it is to get through all the work required of you, but you will save yourself time if you can help your students develop the ability to speed read, to plan and structure essays, to use their examination time effectively, and so on. Although different subject areas will require different types of skills, I would like to offer you a few suggestions that should be applicable to most of the curriculum. There are various books available on the subject of how to study effectively which cover these ideas in much more detail.

Speed or skim reading

The skill of speed reading takes time to learn and master, but you can certainly offer your students a condensed version. Put simply, the idea behind speed reading is that we are taught to read by sounding words out, first aloud and then in our heads. This is what slows us down, as it takes time to read in this way. Our brains are quite capable of seeing, processing and understanding language without having to 'hear' it as well.

A good way to encourage your students to speed up their reading is to teach them to skim passages. Ask them to pick out the important words in a section of text, but give them only a few seconds to look at each page or paragraph. They will discover, much to their surprise, that this is actually quite easy to do. By picking out the 'big' words, such as technical terms and important nouns, it is possible to make sense of a passage in a short space of time.

Mind mapping

This is an excellent technique, which is closely related to brainstorming, but takes a more advanced form. It teaches students to structure their work and start to link ideas and themes together. You can use it in a variety of ways and for many different subjects, for example, history, geography, science and languages. The students brainstorm ideas on a topic or theme, but in no particular order. This is where the mind map comes in – the students must draw out the ideas, putting closely related concepts together and using arrows to link those that have some sort of relationship. They can develop the mind map further by the use of colours, which they can use to differentiate between ideas, and also to represent them. For instance, blue could be used for words connected to water in a geographical mind map.

How to memorize

Again, there are many excellent books that cover memory systems in more detail, but people seem to be wary of using them. Brief details are given in Chapter 3 in 'Learning names', but this is by no means the only use for memory systems. The basic idea is to make connections, again the way the human mind works, to aid memory. After making a mind map for each revision subject, your students should pick out the most important words that will give them access to many other ideas. They can then link these important words together and memorize them (see Chapter 3 for ideas on how to do this).

How to pass exams

In the majority of subjects GCSE and A level students will have to take a written exam, or exams, at the end of their course. This is an area where many of them will face difficulties, often because of a lack of preparation. Examination practice should therefore play an integral part in your teaching, and you should try to replicate exam conditions as fully as you can when setting test papers. If essay writing plays an important role in your subject, then teach your students how to plan their answers before they start writing.

A lot of students have difficulties with timing when they take exams and it is vital to teach them how to use their time effectively. Although it may seem obvious, many students do not realize that they should allocate their time according to how many marks each answer is worth. Students often feel, probably because of nerves, that the more they write the more marks they will gain. Again, it is worth spending time showing them what a model answer in your subject would be.

THE DREADED DIFFERENTIATION

In my opinion differentiation is rather like close marking (see Chapter 7); all very well in theory, but not exactly practical for the working teacher. No doubt you will have explored all the types of differentiation at college, and tried them out with your classes. However, you now have a 'real' job and all the extras that come with it: a full timetable, marking to complete, reports to write, forms to fill out, parents' evenings and meetings to attend, and so on. Realistically, you will have little time to differentiate the work you set, unless you are willing to plan and prepare resources until midnight every night.

In reality, much of the differentiation that takes place in schools is by outcome, i.e. by what the students produce. If you do have a wide range of abilities in your class or classes, you will certainly have to produce a variety of tasks. However, do not be too hard on yourself over this. You will be serving your students far better if you spend your time marking their work carefully and giving them as much individual help as you can. If you do have support teachers, you may find that they can suggest differentiated tasks for the students they are working with.

FINDING RESOURCES

When you start at your school, check on the resources that are already available in your department. You may find that they are very useful to you and save you replicating work that others have already done. However, you may equally well find that they consist of outdated worksheets or textbooks that are difficult to access and impossible to use effectively.

It could be more useful for you to ask other teachers in your department or area if they have any recently prepared resources on the subjects you are covering. Teachers are usually flattered and keen to offer good material if you are enthusiastic and if you are willing to give your own ideas in return. Do try to present any worksheets you make as effectively as you possibly can, preferably in a typed format and with illustrations. This will encourage the students to use them properly.

Remember, too, that resources come in many shapes and sizes. Basically, a resource is anything that the teacher can bring into their lessons to aid the students' understanding of a subject. Students respond particularly well to unusual resources that challenge their creativity and imagination. Here are some ideas for original resources that you could use.

Other teachers

Other teachers can be a very useful resource for you – either the experience and information they can offer which you could use in your lessons, or (if they are willing) they might actually come into your lesson themselves. For instance, you may be a geography or science teacher teaching your students how to draw diagrams, but you may not feel very confident about your own artistic skills. You could perhaps ask an art or design teacher to come into your lessons to demonstrate how to make a good technical drawing. You could then offer them an area of specialism of your own in return.

Other adults

It is rare, particularly in secondary schools, for teachers to invite other adults into their classes. This is a shame, as the students will respond very well to someone they have not met before who is an expert, perhaps a poet or an astronomer. Find out if the parents or guardians of your students (or other adults that you know or could approach) are willing to come in and take a lesson or lessons with your class.

As well as bringing in interesting and often exciting information, other adults provide excellent role models for your students. You could find a female bricklayer or a male dressmaker to challenge stereotypes. Other adults can provide important role models for both male and female students. Seeing adults who have other jobs (i.e. other than teachers) can give your students something concrete to aim for.

Other students

If you have a sixth form in your school, why not approach some of these older students to come and assist you in the classroom? Again, students seem to respond well to non-teachers in the classroom. You could perhaps ask a sixth-former to work with a small group of students, or even one individual student who needs extra help and attention.

Objects

Students seem to respond very well to a teacher who brings objects, unusual or even common, into the classroom. Of course, science, art and technology teachers use a variety of objects in their lessons, but this is by no means the only time they can be used. For instance, an English teacher working on *Romeo and Juliet* could bring in the 'evidence' found at the murder scene. This would include the poison taken by Juliet, the Friar's letter to Romeo, and so on. The students could then examine the 'evidence' as detectives, and try and work out what has happened. Similarly, a language teacher may obtain a more positive response if they set up a market in their classroom and ask the students to buy different types of food using the correct vocabulary.

The library/the Internet

The library and any available CD ROMs or the Internet are, of course, very useful resources for the students. Again, they will respond very well to something they see as unusual. Embarrassingly, you will probably find that the students are far more at home with the latest technology than you are.

USING DISPLAYS

Classroom displays are an essential part of the learning experience for your students: they celebrate the students' work and provide information on a variety of topics. They do take time to prepare and present, but I feel strongly that they are very worth while.

I would like to offer a few thoughts and ideas about displays for you to consider. Many of these comments are perhaps idealistic – busy teachers will have other things on their mind apart from creating display work. However, it is all part of creating a good working environment for your students and they will respond far better to your lessons (and give you an easier time) if they feel you really care about what they are doing and where they have to work.

Change the displays regularly

One of the worst sights in a classroom is a display which is torn, falling down and has graffiti on it. In this instance it would be better for there to be no displays at all. If at all possible, change your displays every half-term, or at least every term. Perhaps use a system of rotation where you always have one class working on creating a display and you take down the oldest or tattiest display to make room for the new one. Even if the room is not 'yours', the students will respond very well to seeing that you value their work by displaying it on the wall. They will be proud of it and other groups will probably express an interest in what they have been doing.

Avoid 'wallpaper' displays

This is not to say that you should view displays as 'wallpaper' – something put up to decorate the walls (or hide their condition). In some schools, as an open evening approaches, or as the arrival of inspectors becomes imminent, a frenzy of display work takes place, display work which then stays up for the rest of the school year. However, your students will recognize this type of display for what it is: a promotion for the school rather than for their benefit. Display work should always be a celebration of what is *currently* going on in the classroom. It will take a while for you to fill your walls at the start of term, but this is not a problem.

Make it worth while

Only put up work that is worth displaying, perhaps because it is artistically attractive, or because it is worth reading. Try not to put up lots of copies of very similar things, for instance a whole class worth of the same piece of work. However, do try and display the work of weaker students, as well as the more able, as this will motivate them. You could help a student redraft a piece for display if, say, they had a problem with spelling.

Interactive displays

Try and make your displays interactive or perhaps three-dimensional. This encourages the students to respond to the displays in a positive way. For instance, displays that include questions will invite a response, as will displays that have lift-up flaps. There are many opportunities for creating three-dimensional displays. For instance, a science teacher could make models of the planets and create a solar system; a drama teacher could get the students to make masks; a history teacher could have a display based around fireworks night which includes fireworks made using cardboard rolls. If you don't have any ideas of your own, ask an art teacher or the students themselves for some suggestions.

By and for the students

I am all too aware of the temptation to put the displays up yourself, to ensure that they are neat. However, do bear in mind that displays will elicit a more positive response if the students feel that they have created them themselves. If your students are not old enough or capable enough, you could act as an 'artistic director'. By allowing the students to take control, you will also save yourself time. There is no reason why displays should not go up within lesson time, if you have the space to do this.

Part of the learning experience

Always treat a display as part of the students' education. This will happen fairly automatically if it is connected closely to the work they are doing. Do not feel that a display always comes at the end of a topic or subject, as a demonstration of what has been learned. It can also come at or near the beginning of a unit of work, so that you can refer to it during your lessons. Of course, a display can also include preprinted material. For instance, a map of your local area will be very helpful to a geography teacher as the class works on a project studying the immediate environment.

A motivating factor

There is something very rewarding about seeing a piece of work that you have done being displayed on a wall for everyone to see. Try putting yourself in the student's shoes and thinking about how good this would make you feel. You will not only motivate the students whose work is on the wall, but also the rest of the class and other students who use the room.

Keep displays tidy

As I have said previously, there is nothing worse than a 'tatty' display. It is worth taking a few moments whenever you think about it to tidy up the displays in your room(s). It can be disheartening when students do not treat displays with the respect they deserve, but at least it shows them interacting with the work. By their very nature, displays will become damaged as the students bump into them. There also seems to be a strong compulsion among some students to purloin drawing pins and Blutack: I am not entirely sure what they actually do with them. There are two solutions to this: use a staple-gun if you have one, or replace the pins regularly.

TAKING CARE OF YOURSELF

In many ways, teaching is like acting. You are 'performing' to an audience (your students) and you have to be 'in character' as a teacher all (or most) of the time. There will be times when you do not feel like playing your part, but you have no choice – the audience of students are there and waiting for your instructions or your words of wisdom. This can become very tiring: after all, no actor is expected to perform on stage for over 5 hours a day, every day of the week. How, then, can you prevent the inevitable tiredness that you will experience? Here are some ideas.

Take your breaks

The temptation to work through break-time and lunch is incredibly strong and I can easily see why some teachers do this. You know that the work you have to do (and there is *always* work waiting to be done) will still be there after school, so why not try to get some of it done in your breaks so you can go home earlier? You may have detentions that have to be supervised, or students who need to talk to you about a problem, or a piece of coursework. When else are you supposed to do this?

I suggest that you are ruthless with yourself about this one. If at all possible, make a point of going for a coffee in the staff room before school starts, getting there during break-time and always having as full a lunch-time as you can. There are two main reasons for this. First and foremost, you need to give yourself the opportunity to rest during the day. You will not serve your students to the best of your ability if you are tired and irritable. Second, and perhaps equally important, you need to spend time with other teachers. As I pointed out in Chapter 1, the other staff in the school are a vital part of your support system and there is little chance to get to know them unless you go to the staff room. It is also good for you to have some adult company, a chance to have a laugh or a moan. Rest time is *never* wasted time.

Take sick leave

If you are ill, *do not* come into school. I have covered this idea in Chapter 1, but I will happily repeat it. You are not indispensable, you do not want to pass on your illness to other teachers, you *can* afford to take a day off. If you know in advance that you are going to need a day off, for instance if you feel progressively sicker during the day, then if you really have to, take some marking home with you so you do not get too far behind.

Be a quiet teacher

A violinist's tool is their violin, which can be replaced if it gets broken. As I have said, you are more like an actor – your voice is your tool and you must take care of it. Avoid shouting at all costs, talk as quietly as you can and try to avoid the 'chalk and talk' style of teaching, where you are required to talk a great deal. Make your students do the work as often as you can. Remember, 'quiet teachers get quiet classes' (see Chapter 3).

Make the most of your holidays

One of the best perks of a teaching job is undoubtedly the holidays, so use them for the most appropriate reason – to take a break. At the end of term you will feel exhausted, both emotionally and physically. Try to avoid the overwhelming temptation to catch up on all that marking and planning you never have time to do. Remember, your job will expand to fit the amount of time you are willing to devote to it. Be ruthless with yourself and plan lots of lovely holidays (if you can afford them). You will feel better for it.

Chapter 5

The Role of the Form Tutor

WHAT IS A FORM TUTOR?

Alongside your job as a subject teacher, you may well be asked to take responsibility for a tutor group, also known as a form or registration class. The role of a form tutor is essentially to take care of the 'whole' student. Your administrative responsibilities will include taking the register, which is (perhaps surprisingly) a legal document that you must fill out correctly (see the following section in this chapter). You will probably also be required to check and collate reports for your form. Some schools assign a co-tutor to inexperienced teachers, and this person will be able to answer many of your questions.

The form tutor has overall responsibility for a group of students and may start with a group of students when they enter a school, moving up with them as the years pass. Apart from the administrative responsibilities that the role of form tutor entails, you will also need to keep a check on how your students are performing in their different subjects, taking an overview of their progress at school. As with much of the job of a teacher, the role expands to meet the amount of time you are willing to devote to it, but being an efficient and caring tutor brings its own rewards. You may find that you do not actually teach any of the students in your form, particularly in their first year at school. This is probably beneficial, as it means you can develop a strong relationship with them that is unrelated to their lesson time.

In some schools the form tutor is also responsible for teaching personal and social education (PSE) to their group. If this is the case, you will have the opportunity to spend more time with the students, get to know them better, and also explore some of the issues that may be troubling them. Registration periods can often get eaten up by administration, particularly at the beginning of term. In some schools, however, a fairly long period of time is assigned for registration and other activities associated with the form group.

YOUR RESPONSIBILITIES

First-year students

If you have a first-year group, your main responsibility at the beginning of term will be to ensure that they settle in and have all the information that they need. Some of them will need reassurance as starting at a new school can be a traumatic experience. They will be unsure of the layout of the buildings, but your school should issue you with maps that you can go through with your students. This will help you as well in the difficult task of finding your way around. Make sure that they know the location of the most important areas: the form room, the assembly hall, the student reception, and so on. The students will also receive timetables and it is important that they understand how these work. One of the biggest changes for students starting at a secondary school is the fact that they have so many different subjects, with a different teacher and a different classroom for each one.

If your school uses student diaries, you will have to hand these out and explain to the students how to use them, so make sure you take a good look at one before you start. Ensure that you give them time to write or stick their timetables into their diaries, so they do not get lost. You should receive two copies of each timetable, one to give to the students and one for your own reference. You may find that you have to collect money for various activities. You will probably also be asked to get your students to fill out an information form, which will give you invaluable details about addresses, names of parents or guardians, telephone numbers, dates of birth and so on.

Some secondary schools have a staggered start to the first term, so that the new students have a chance to find their feet before the older ones return. You will hopefully get an extended period of time at the beginning of the year so that you can deal with all these additional jobs.

Finding out about your students

Some of your students may have special educational needs (SEN) and it is important that you find out about this as soon as possible. There is more information about this in Chapter 9. You could also chat to your head of year or house who should have material on the students from their previous schools (or, if they are not first years, from previous years at your school). You should avoid judging your students solely on this information, but there may be special home circumstances that it is essential for you to know about and take into account. You may also need to notify subject teachers about any specific requirements or difficulties with a particular student.

During the year, you could be asked to assess those students in your group who have low-level special needs. This assessment may involve simply checking their progress by looking carefully at their subject reports. If you do come across any students who are struggling in some or all of their lessons, you should notify the special needs department as soon as possible.

The register

As mentioned previously, the register is a legal document. If you are lucky, you may find that the office staff at your school have filled in the dates for you. If not, you will need to do this yourself, but you should be very careful not to make a mistake. Ask an experienced member of staff (or someone in the school office) if you are not sure. You should include half-terms and training days in your dates. When you are taking the register, a student is either absent (marked with a blank circle) or present (marked with a line). Check before starting to see what colour pens your school wants you to use in the register.

When a student has been absent, you must obtain confirmation of this absence from their parents or guardians and a reason for it. In the front of your register you will find a list of letters to use for the different types of absence. In the majority of cases, the parents or guardians will send in a letter with the student, but if absence is not authorized almost immediately, you may find it easier to telephone their home. Some schools have a standard letter for you to send home asking the parents or guardians to explain absences.

Using your register, watch for any students who display a particular pattern of absence or who are missing a great deal of school. You should also watch for possible cases of truancy. If this happens, or if you have any suspicions, notify your head of year or house and the special needs department.

Depending on the size and structure of your school, you will probably have an assembly with your year or house group on at least one day a week. You may be asked to take the register during this assembly. As with your classes, it is very useful to have your students sitting in alphabetical order for this. You will find it much easier to mark them in and you can also start learning their names: a real difficulty if you do not actually teach them. (See Chapter 3, section on 'Learning names', for more ideas on how to do this.)

The student diary

Many schools now use student diaries and they are a really useful way of communicating with parents or guardians and other teachers. Students can write down their homework in them and their teachers can enter detentions. Unfortunately, this system is open to abuse: diaries are 'lost' when the detention pages are full; some students manage to get themselves two diaries. The school will usually ask the student's parents or guardians to check the diaries and sign them. Again, although in theory this is a useful device, it is not difficult for the students to perfect a forged signature.

Try to have a regular time and day when you check diaries, perhaps during an assembly if you have one. Check the detention page, as well as ensuring that the parent or guardian has seen and signed the diary. If a student is receiving a lot of detentions, find a time early on to talk to them about why this is happening. Is there a particular pattern of behaviour developing, or do they appear to have a problem with a specific subject or teacher? If a student is not recording homework in sufficient detail, or is not being set much homework, you should talk to them about this as well.

Contact with parents or guardians

It is often the case that secondary school teachers have very little contact with the student's home, apart from through letters and student diaries. As a form tutor you may well find that you only ever speak to parents or guardians on the phone, or perhaps meet them at parents' evenings. Your school may organize an information evening for new students, and this can be a very worthwhile way of meeting their parents or guardians. You will also be communicating with them through subject reports, but at best you can form only a superficial relationship.

Reports

One of the more time-consuming aspects of the role of a form tutor comes when reports are due. Tutors are usually responsible for correlating and proofreading all the different subject reports, as well as making their own overall comment about each student's progress. The reason this can take so much time is because you may need to have reports sent back and amended, or you may not receive reports at all from some teachers, and you will need to remind them. Unfortunately, there is not a great deal you can do about this. Do remember, however, the trouble this causes you and when you are doing reports for other year groups try to hand them in on time and ensure that they are correct the first time around. You will save yourself, as well as other teachers, a lot of time and effort if you do this.

The completed reports will usually be checked by a head of year, a deputy head or other senior manager. They will then be given to the students, or alternatively posted to the home. You may be asked to obtain return slips from your form, confirming receipt of the report. If there are any students who have proved particularly unreliable (or who have a very poor report that they might not want their parents or guardians to read), it might be best to ensure the report is posted home, rather than given to the student.

Social and personal issues

One of the most important (and satisfying) parts of being a form tutor is dealing with any social and personal issues that arise with your students. The more serious issues, for instance any special educational needs or bullying incidents, should always be dealt with in partnership with more experienced or senior teachers. However, there will be occasions when a student simply needs to talk to someone about something that is worrying them.

At the start of your time with the form group, make it clear that they can come and talk to you privately if they ever need your help. They may feel closer to a subject teacher, that they spend more time with in school, but if they do come to you always try and make time to talk to them. If it is not possible for this to happen during registration time, let them know where you will be at break-time or after school. Often a student will just want someone to listen to their problems, a shoulder to cry on. At other times you may feel that you cannot deal with their problem effectively on your own, in which case you could refer them to a more senior member of staff, or to a school counsellor if you have one.

Try to give your form the sense that you care about how they behave in all their lessons and that you really want them to succeed at school. In many ways you can act as a neutral observer and offer them an overview of their behaviour at school. For instance, if one of your students is getting into trouble with teachers because of their confrontational behaviour, you may be able to point this out to them without making them feel angry. This is especially the case if you do not actually teach them.

The role of your pastoral manager

As a form tutor you have limited responsibility, particularly for the more serious issues that arise. Your pastoral manager, probably a head of year or head of house, is being paid to deal with the group of students as a whole. If you refer such problems to him or her you are discharging your own duty adequately. A written referral is helpful for the pastoral manager, rather than simply having a chat during a spare moment. In this way they will have the evidence they need to take the matter further and they will be able to deal with the problem in their own time.

You should do the best job you can with your form group, but be careful not to take on extra work that is not really yours, particularly when you are just starting out as a teacher. You may wish to attend any special needs meetings that concern a student from your group, as these will give you additional insight into their problems, but there is no compulsion for you to do so.

DEVELOPING YOUR ROLE

It really is up to you how far you want to take your role. There are various ways of motivating your form group and making them feel like a team. These include creating competitions to see who can achieve the most merit marks, or whatever reward system your school uses. You may also find that your school runs its own competitions, for instance to sell tickets to a Christmas market or a noticeboard competition for each year or house group. There might also be competition between the form groups to see who has the best attendance and punctuality records.

A good way to motivate your group and keep them up to date with information is to keep a well-organized noticeboard. Depending on the age of the students, they could design and make this themselves, or with your help. The noticeboard could include your name, the name of your form group, a list of the school rules, names of the students in the group, their 'baby pictures', and so on.

An effective way to make your form feel that you really care about them would be to give birthday cards. This is fairly straightforward as you will have their dates of birth in the register. There are two drawbacks with this idea: the first is that you will have to buy or make the cards yourself, the second is that you must remember to give every single student a card, or they will be very disappointed.

Finally, one of the most time-consuming administrative tasks in a form group is getting them to hand things in, for instance return slips on reports, absence letters, and so on. You could motivate them to do this in various ways: one way is to give merits (or some other reward) to those who hand notes in the next day; another way is to give out detentions if they do not, but remember that you will have to take the detention.

Part II

Climbing the Paper Mountain

Chapter 6

Paperwork

Amazingly, one of the hardest tasks teachers face is to deal with the mountains of paper that pass through their hands. Whole forests of trees are felled each year to create the masses of paperwork that teachers have to fight their way through. Of course, some of this paperwork is vital, for instance reports and SEN forms. Some of it (a lot of it) is created specially for you by government departments. Unfortunately it is also true that the school for which you work will be a willing participant in adding to your work-load.

How, then, do you deal with this potentially time-wasting aspect of the job? This chapter is a short one – I would like to avoid adding further to your workload. The following three rules should cover most eventualities.

THE FIRST RULE: 'B' IS FOR BIN

You should apply this rule to every piece of paper that you receive, and if you follow it as ruthlessly as you can, your pile of important paperwork will stay quite small. The rule goes as follows: as each piece of paper arrives in your pigeon-hole, ask yourself the question, *'Does the thought of throwing this away make me want to cry?'* If the answer is *'No'*, then throw it away immediately. If you do make a mistake and throw away something important, someone else will always have a copy.

There are many examples of paper that can end up in the bin. For instance, after reading the agenda for a meeting and attending the meeting itself, there is little point in keeping your copy of the agenda. Similarly, if there is centralized documentation that is easily accessible, you will not need to keep copies of your own. Examples might include department handbooks, duty rotas and so on.

When (and if) you receive a list of departmental resources, bear the following in mind: there may be useful resources within your department that would save you from making your own, but then again they may be dated or poorly presented. There is never much spare time in teaching to sort through filing cabinets and, consequently, a lot of unused and worthless paper tends to build up. So, if you know this applies to your department's resources, the list can go straight in the bin.

THE SECOND RULE: FILE IT, DEAL WITH IT, PASS IT ON

You should apply this rule to all the paper that you have left over after following the first rule. So, once you have weeded out the non-essential paperwork, what do you do with what is left? There are three options to consider: file it, deal with it or pass it on.

1. *File it.* Be wary of this one. The phrase 'I might use it or need it again' is the way those mountains of paper start to build up. File *only* what is essential (see 'The third rule' below to find out how to decide what to file).
2. *Deal with it.* The best option, faced with any piece of paper that requires a response or action of some type is to deal with it straightaway, as soon as you take it out of your pigeon-hole. That way you can move straight on to option (3) with the leftovers. If you don't feel confident about dealing with it, check immediately with somebody else what you should do. If you feel the piece of paper requires a more considered response, by all means take your time, but avoid having a pile of papers known as 'to be done'. When, exactly, are you going to 'do' them?
3. *Pass it on.* Always the preferred option, as it ensures your paperwork becomes somebody else's problem. Whenever possible, for instance when filling out special needs forms, do not agonize about what you are going to write. Fill the form in that instant and then pass it on. It is far better to do this than to be one of those teachers with piles of forms that they will *never* fill in on their desks. If you do it wrong the first time nobody is going to blame you; you have only just started teaching after all, and they can always come back to you if it does need changing.

THE THIRD RULE: WILL I USE IT AGAIN?

Finally, the third rule deals with everything left over after you have followed Rules (1) and (2). Just be honest with yourself. If you have made a photocopiable resource, keep a copy, but make sure it is easily accessible. If it is not, you will end up making it again at some point in the future, so what is the point of keeping it? If you can, file one copy of each worksheet in a plastic folder that you can take out easily to photocopy. When filing, it is useful to have your resources divided into different topics and also into different year groups.

If you have access to a computer of your own, this is the ideal way to store your resources, as it makes searching for and printing them out a very simple task. However, be wary of storing resources on a school computer: they may well disappear or at the very least get lost among the work of other teachers.

Chapter 7

Marking and Exams

MARKING: A BALANCING ACT

Marking is, like many aspects of teaching, a job that expands to meet the amount of time you are willing (or able) to devote to it. On teaching practice, it is likely that your timetable was only a fraction of that of a full-time teacher and you had plenty of (or at least enough) time for planning and checking your students' work. Now you have to deal not only with teaching and marking, but also with all the other administrative tasks that come with the job, including writing reports and attending meetings. It is now that you find out just how much of a balancing act marking really is.

You will no doubt have heard complaints from those outside the teaching profession that teachers 'do not bother' to correct mistakes in their students' work. This, of course, is not necessarily true. It is more likely a result of the fact that close marking (see the following section in this chapter) takes a great deal of time. If a teacher were to close mark a three-page piece of work, adding lots of comments and corrections, it could take them up to half an hour (depending, of course, on the subject being marked). Multiply this by an average of 25 or 30 students in a class, then by the number of classes the teacher has (perhaps ten to fifteen depending on the subject) and you can see why this is practically impossible. Teachers may have a shorter working day than other professionals, but a marking load of over 100 hours a week is not realistic.

Teachers have to take some difficult decisions about marking. They must decide how to balance the importance of checking work with the equal necessity to plan lessons, make resources, create displays, and so on. They must also decide which of their classes should take priority: for instance, coursework from an examination year class needs to be checked carefully. There is no way that you can complete this type of marking at school and so you must decide whether you are willing to spend evenings and weekends finishing it. This is the reality of the balancing act that is marking.

THE OPTIONS

Teachers are, of course, individuals who mark work in a wide variety of ways. The marking style you choose also depends very much on the subject you are teaching: a history or geography project will obviously be marked very differently to a piece of art work or a scientific analysis. When you start teaching you will probably want to experiment with different methods to see how effective you find each one. Your choice of how to mark will depend, too, on your educational philosophies, the policies of your department or school, and how much time you are willing to spend. However, before you start it is worth exploring a few of the options.

Pencil or pen?

There are various schools of thought on this, but your department will probably have a specific policy that they ask you to follow. I recommend that you question the value of each option and make your own decision. The main points to consider are as follows:

- *Pencil*   Pencil marks are easier to change if you make a mistake but they are harder for the student to see and more vulnerable to alteration. Using a pencil suggests that the teacher's comments or grades are only a subjective judgement rather than a definitive one: the student is not necessarily right or wrong, but the teacher is giving their opinion of the work. This is particularly useful in subjects where the work is imaginative rather than factual. Pencil can be a very useful way of marking important pieces of work, for instance final drafts of examination coursework, as the student can make necessary alterations using correction fluid and then rub the pencil marks out.
- *Pen*   Pen marks are easier for the student to see, but harder for you to change if you make a mistake. Student alterations are practically impossible, although I have seen it done. Using a pen gives a stronger suggestion that the teacher is judging the student's work and is therefore perhaps more suited to subjects that have right and wrong answers. Some students actually feel more comfortable with pen marks, as they *want* the teacher to make a definitive judgement on their work.

Marks, letters, numbers or comments

Again, this will be dependent on your school or departmental policies, and on the subject that you teach. In certain subjects, or for particular pieces of work, it will be possible to give a definitive mark. For instance a series of maths sums or a spelling test can be given a mark that can then be used to check progress across a class of students. However, there will be times when the work you set needs to be given a less objective grading, and this can pose difficulties for the inexperienced teacher.

You may feel that it is less destructive to give a comment on a piece of work rather than a grade, but again I would argue that students want to know where their work stands in relation to others. Giving a letter or number will also allow you to compare a piece of work across the class of students.

You will need to find out whether you are supposed to grade pieces of work in relation to the student, the group, or the year as a whole. For instance, is a grade A in a bottom set the equivalent to a grade A in a top set? If one of your weakest students tries really hard on a particular piece of work, but still produces very poor results, do you really want to demoralize him or her by giving a very low grade? This problem is avoided somewhat by giving two grades, one for effort and one for attainment, a fairly common practice in schools now.

You will also have to come to a decision about how ruthless you are going to be about grading students (both on class work and reports). If a grade E is the lowest grade you can give, and on the report is explained as 'very poor quality of work' or a similarly negative comment, how willing are you going to be to give any student this grade? There is a real dilemma here between being honest (and alerting parents or guardians and special needs teachers to any problems) and destroying a student's confidence.

Tick and flick

This type of marking is exactly as it sounds: a big tick (or cross) on each answer, then move on to the next. At the end of the work there may be a brief comment, such as 'good' or 'a fair attempt', and a grade or mark. Certain subjects or particular pieces of work may demand this type of marking: for instance a series of maths sums or a test on vocabulary learned in language lessons.

In some cases, though, this would not be the appropriate style of marking. For instance, a piece of creative writing or a long and detailed essay could be marked in this way, but it would be a fairly meaningless exercise and would have little value for the student. Similarly, if it was clear that a student doing a maths test had not understood the work, you would probably want to write comments and give examples to show where he or she was going wrong.

Close marking

This is what some people see as the ideal (but as I have explained an unrealistic ideal in the majority of cases). In close marking the teacher pinpoints and corrects every error, writing detailed comments or giving working to show how the answers should be formulated. There are obviously advantages in this method, not least of which is that the student sees exactly where they are going wrong. However, for weaker students this style of marking can be destructive. If a student has worked hard on a piece which is then covered in red ink this would be very demoralizing.

Marking for specific errors

As well as offering a good balance between 'tick and flick' and close marking, this method also encourages the students to focus on correcting their work themselves. With this style of marking the teacher pinpoints one area that they will be marking. Examples would be the correct spelling of certain words (you could give out a list beforehand); showing detailed working (even if the answers are wrong); producing neat diagrams; correct use of technical terminology, and so on. This encourages the student to concentrate on areas of weakness and you can also set different marking targets for different students, depending on their specific problems.

SOME TIME-SAVING TIPS

There is a real temptation to think of marking as something the teacher does after a lesson, for the students to look through and absorb when a piece of work is returned to them. However, there are some very good ways of saving time with marking that are very sound educationally speaking. For instance, students are often aware of the strengths and weaknesses in their own work, but have very little idea of what others in the class are doing. This is a shame, as they can learn a lot from the work of others. I would offer a word of caution, though, before asking students to mark each other's work: this can be demoralizing for any very weak students. You could perhaps 'fix' it so that this work comes to you.

Do-it-yourself

Before you collect in a piece of work, or if a few of your students finish the work you have set early, ask them to check through their work themselves. If you know they have problems in one area, you could ask them to look for a specific type of mistake, for instance to underline any words they think they have misspelt, or circle any technical terms that they believe are used wrongly.

Do-it-together

This is very useful if you are setting a test where the answers are straightforward and can be marked as right or wrong. After the test has finished you go through the answers one by one with the class, perhaps writing them on the board, and ask your students to tick (or cross) their work and give a mark at the end. If it is important that the results are accurate, you could ask the students to swop with a partner to guard against cheating.

What is your opinion?

This technique is useful for pieces of work that call for an opinion rather than a mark, for instance art and design or creative writing. In my experience, although they moan about this exercise, students really enjoy it. When the time for completing a piece of work is up, you ask a few students to collect all the books or papers in and 'shuffle' them, then return them to the class, ensuring that no one gets their own work to mark. For this exercise you should give the students specific areas to mark and you should also let them know what you want the marks to be out of. For instance, you could ask for marks out of ten for creativity, accuracy, originality, and so on. You could also ask them to write a positive comment saying what they liked about the work.

If anyone finishes early, or if you have time, get a second (and third) set of marks and comments from your students by asking them to swop again. They should then return the work to its owner who can read what their peers have put. Students tend to take this exercise seriously, as they like playing the role of teacher and when you collect the work in you will have a ready-made set of comments to assist your own marking. Your students will also learn valuable lessons about the work of their peers and about how difficult your role as a teacher actually is.

Marking in class

In some situations it is possible to mark work in class, perhaps if students are finishing an exercise at different rates or if they are working in silence on a test and you can be sure that they won't start talking or cheating the minute you lower your head. I have found that it is difficult to get any meaningful marking done during lesson time because there are so many interruptions. However, if you do find it possible it will certainly save you some time.

Remember that in some subjects your marking is not just of written pieces, but of oral work as well. You could ask your students to prepare a presentation on a topic during the lesson that you can watch and assess (see Chapter 4, 'Lessons for the tired teacher'). This exercise takes time and is also student, rather than teacher intensive, so it will give you the opportunity to have a rest.

COLLECTING WORK

As I suggested in Chapter 1, you should always ask your students to collect in work for you unless there is a specific reason not to do so, as this will save you time and effort and they will be perfectly willing to help. If you are collecting in homework, one way to ensure that everyone has completed the task you set is to ask the students to have their books in front of them, open at the page where they have done the homework. You can then go around and check before the books are collected in. Any students who do not complete the homework should have their diaries out, so that you can write in the detention they have 'earned' (see Chapter 3).

There is some discussion about when it is best to collect in homework but really it depends very much on the class. If there are going to be confrontations about uncompleted homework, you might be best to wait until the end of the lesson rather than risk disruption, but do make sure you leave yourself enough time to write down detentions. Alternatively, once the students have settled down to work you could go around checking homework and giving out detentions. If the students need to use their exercise books during the lesson, you can collect them in or ask the students to leave them in neat piles at the end of the class.

KEEPING MARKS

It is important to keep a record of the marks achieved by your students, so that when you come to write reports or attend a parents' evening, you have the information at hand. (Inspectors will also want to see detailed information about grades and marks.)

It is very much a matter of personal taste how you do this, but I would suggest that rather than have a mark book you keep them in your teacher's planner (see Chapter 2) on a separate page to your class register, but in the same section as the class they relate to. The reason for this is so that you have a line of marks for each student that give an immediate overview of progress (or lack of it). Because they are in the same place as your register, it will be easy to verify whether a student was present or absent from the lesson when checking off homework.

SOME TIPS ON EXAMS

Unless your timetable requires you to take on an examination class who are half-way through their course, it is unlikely that you will have to worry about public examinations in your first year of teaching. However, if you teach examination groups that are in the first year of a two-year course, you will need to plan ahead. Another concern is the standardized tests that take place during the year for students who have reached the end of a key stage. It is worth spending some time considering how best to help your students do well in these exams. Although it may seem unfair, one of the ways that your success as a teacher will be judged is through the examination results your students achieve.

Preparing your students

It is essential that you prepare your students exactly for the syllabus or tests they are doing, so check carefully and well in advance what they must do. If you are uncertain about any aspects, ask a more experienced member of staff. Look at past exam papers to see what type of questions are likely to come up. Exams sometimes follow a very similar format from year to year, and you may be able to calculate which subjects are likely to come up by looking at previous papers.

Spend lots of time getting your students to take mock exams, either practical or written depending on your subject. This is important because it will train them to work quickly – one of the most useful skills in an examination – and also because it will show them just how hard (and long) exams can be. They must also learn to get the timing right – point out to them that the examiner will give marks for each answer and if they do not complete the paper they will not gain any marks for the uncompleted sections. Try as well to persuade them not to 'waffle' or to give unnecessary detail. Passing exams is often a case of simply answering the questions clearly and concisely. There is a great temptation for students to feel that the more they write, the better they will do.

Coursework

External examinations, depending on the syllabus you are studying and the subject you are teaching, may be made up of coursework and a final paper or papers. If coursework does play a part in your syllabus, ask your head of department for advice and find out the deadlines for handing in essays or projects. You may find that some of your students have difficulty in completing coursework, but bear in mind that something is better than nothing and even if they have not managed to produce a finished piece of work, you should still be able to find something to enter. A student will often be withdrawn from the exam if they do not enter all the coursework required.

What to take to the exams

Ensure that your students know exactly what they must take to their exams. If your syllabus allows them to take in additional aids, then make sure that they do so: a calculator to their maths exam; a dictionary to their languages exam; copies of their set texts to their literature exam. Any student who does not have access to this equipment will be severely disadvantaged.

How to pass exams

It is worth training your students in the skills they will need to pass and do well in their exams: what and how to revise, any necessary preparatory work, how to use their time effectively, both in revision and in the exams themselves. Teach them, too, any skills that are specific to your subject: how to write essays, how to draw clear diagrams, how much working to show in analytical answers, etc. You will know much better than they do exactly what the examiners will be looking for. There is more information on useful skills to teach your classes in Chapter 4. Remember, you can train even the less able students to succeed if they know how to revise and how to sit their exams.

INVIGILATION

Think of the most boring thing you can imagine in the whole world, multiply it by twenty, and you have some idea of how boring invigilation is. The summer arrives and you think: '*Great, my GCSE classes are off on study leave, at last I'll be able to catch up on all that paperwork.*' Think again. Now is the time of year when all your free lessons (i.e. those frees created by classes on study leave) are likely to be taken up by invigilation. You must stand in the hall or gym (or wherever the public examinations are taking place) and watch a large group of students for the duration of your normal lesson time. You cannot do marking or planning during this time, but are required to walk up and down the rows, checking that the students are not cheating and answering any queries.

Some of the more imaginative teachers I have met come up with various ways of making time pass quickly, and I shall leave it to you to see how inventive you can be. One word of warning: although it is rare to see members of the senior management invigilating (they *know* how boring it is, and anyway, they are far too busy running the school), you may find that from time to time the head or a deputy head pops in to see how the students (and teachers) are doing. At this point, you should make a determined effort to look really engrossed in the thrilling task of invigilation. Good luck!

PREDICTED GRADES

It is highly likely that, after marking mock examinations, you will have to predict the grades that your students should achieve in their real exams. This information will help towards accepting or rejecting students from entry to a sixth form, or may be used to help with university applications. This is not likely to affect you in your first year of teaching, unless you teach an examination class that is half-way through its course. However, I would like to give you a few thoughts and ideas on predicted grades.

Make sure that you base your prediction both on the mock grade and on your classroom teaching, but bear in mind that students will often have improved by the end of the year and also that some will not perform as expected in their exams because of nerves. These factors will mean that your predictions can only ever be an estimate. In some subjects your students may have already handed in finished pieces of coursework or projects, so try to account for the grades they are likely to achieve for those as well.

Chapter 8

Assessment and Reporting

IDEAS FOR ASSESSMENT

In Chapter 7 there are many ideas about *how* to mark students' work, but you will also need to decide *what* you want to assess. It would be a difficult task for any teacher to fully assess every piece of work for every student and I would suggest that it is better, therefore, to take more time over assessing specific tasks. In this way, you can see how the student stands in relation to the rest of the class and you can ensure that you cover all the necessary areas of assessment for your subject.

Assessment will vary widely from subject to subject, and your school or department may have a list of activities or tasks that they want you to assess. If you are left to your own devices in deciding what to assess, do ensure that you cover all the different areas of your subject. You may be asked to collect evidence of your assessment: written pieces, art work, computer-based activities, and even tapes or videos of oral work.

You will find that you are constantly performing assessments of the students you teach during the course of each lesson, even though they are not formalized or written down. You will be noticing who needs help with spelling, who finds it hard to offer ideas to the class, who has poor co-ordination skills, who has difficulty with mathematical concepts, and so on.

THE IMPORTANCE OF SPECIAL EDUCATIONAL NEEDS

It is during this informal assessment that you may first notice the special educational needs of some of your students. Some of these students will have been identified already, but it is by no means certain that all of them will. As an inexperienced teacher, you may be unsure of the process that your school uses if a student has some sort of special educational need. However, I would urge you to take the time to find out, and to follow the process as soon as you spot someone who you feel needs a formal assessment. The process should normally be fairly simple, perhaps a brief form that asks you to state your areas of concern.

It is very hard for a special needs department to identify students needing special help who have so far remained unidentified. Often SEN staff will not do a great deal of normal classroom teaching, but will spend their time helping and supporting the students whose needs they know about already. Obviously, some students will slip through the net, or will develop special needs (for instance behavioural problems) as they grow older. Do not imagine that, if you do not identify a student you feel needs help, someone else will do it. It may be that the student has a specific difficulty that is only noticeable in your particular subject area. The form tutor (see Chapter 5) has a role to play, but if they do not teach the student they will remain unaware of the problems until report time comes around.

SOME TIPS ON WRITING REPORTS

Reporting to parents and guardians takes many different forms: from an informal chat on the telephone to the more formalized written reports and parents evenings. Schools use a very wide range of formats and styles for their written reports. Some use a computerized bank of statements for each subject that the teacher can choose from; some use a combination of tick boxes or statements for specific subject skills alongside a written teacher comment; others require the teacher to devise comments of their own. The ideas and suggestions in this and the following two sections will be of most use to teachers who have to provide their own statements. If your school uses a computerized format for their reports, you could look through the phrases given in 'Some useful phrases for reports' and ask your head of department to add some of them to your own bank of comments.

The idea of a report is to communicate to the parents or guardians, as clearly and concisely as you can, how a student is performing in your subject. A good report will also include strategies for improvement and some specific targets for the student to focus on: words such as 'aim', 'ensure', 'develop' and so on are useful here. The report is one of the main forms of communication between the school and the home. You should therefore make sure that you present it neatly and think carefully about what you are going to say. Your school will have its own rules for written reports, but generally you will find that you are required to write in black ink rather than blue, and that you are not allowed to use correction fluid on your reports (see the following section for short cuts here). Remember, a member of the senior management may check your reports, so ensure that you make a good impression.

In 'Some useful phrases for reports' you will find a list of phrases that you may find helpful when you come to write your reports. I would also strongly urge you to put at least one personalized comment on each report. As you will see from the comments there is no need to use overly technical or complicated language, indeed you should avoid doing this if possible. The recipients of the report will come from a variety of backgrounds and will all need to understand what the teacher is saying. You should therefore avoid unnecessarily complicated vocabulary, as well as avoiding the use of slang and abbreviations. This, unfortunately, is easier said than done.

As well as setting targets for improvement, it is also important that you give the parents or guardians honest information on how the student is progressing. Having said this, you should always try to stress the positive. This means phrasing what you write in such a way as to encourage, rather than demotivate, the student. For instance, a negative, poorly written report (although rather overexaggerated) might say: '*Johnny can't concentrate for longer than a few minutes and he's always ruining my lessons by chatting to his mates.*' A more positive version of this, which also incorporates some targets for the student, could say: '*Although he tries hard, Johnny does find it difficult to maintain his concentration for extended periods of time. He should aim to avoid being distracted by other students in the class.*'

There will be occasions where you find it almost impossible to say anything positive about a student. Do bear in mind that a student who is proving this difficult to teach will be (or should be) receiving help from special needs teachers. Unless you feel very strongly about 'having your say', do try to be positive in the way that you phrase your report. The parents or guardians, and indeed the student, will no doubt be receiving very negative comments in many subjects. This may well lead to even greater alienation from school. You must achieve a balance between honesty and subtlety.

SHORT CUTS TO WRITING REPORTS

In some subjects the teacher faces the prospect of writing reports on students that they may not know at all well. They may only see each class once a week, for instance if they teach a subject like music, drama or art, and this will make identifying (let alone assessing) the students a nightmare. This is particularly so for reports that come near the beginning of the year. You may find that you teach five classes in a particular year group, and when report time comes around you have approximately 150 different reports to write. Do try to plan in advance for this eventuality and start these reports as early as you can. Remember, even if your school uses a computerized format, it will still take you a long time to choose comments and print out the reports.

I would urge you very, very strongly to hand in your reports on time. Chapter 5 gives some of the reasons for this. There is nothing more infuriating (or unprofessional, for that matter) to have to chase a teacher for a set of reports they should have handed in a week ago. The names of teachers who never file their reports on time will be well known in your staff room. Do not add your name to the list!

In order to help you avoid this, there are some short cuts you can take, which should not affect the quality of your reports too greatly. These short cuts are particularly applicable to the teacher who sees lots of different classes in one year group. If you teach a subject where you see the students three times a week, you should be able to give rather more individualized reports, and I would recommend that you do so. Although reports are obviously important, there is (and always will be) a great variation in the quality of different subject reports in a secondary school. You will have to balance your desire for the students' parents or guardians to feel that you are a very caring and efficient teacher, with the need to get the reports done (and handed in) in a realistic amount of time. Do not worry about using these short cuts if they prove necessary.

First, a good short cut is to group your students into types, basically the weakest, the average and the good. You could stretch this to five categories if you wanted to include those with special problems and the really excellent students. You should then find three or four general statements that cover each of these categories, giving one personalized statement for each student. This would be particularly easy to do if your school does use the computerized bank of statements.

Even if you are asked to devise your own reports, access to a computer can greatly speed up the process, as you can feed each category of reports through the printer. Simply take your general statements, add one personal one at the beginning, and print them out. Do be careful, however, that you have not made any mistakes in your general statements. If you have, you will have to reprint or correct the whole set. Be careful, also, to change the gender on the report as appropriate.

When producing handwritten reports, always use a black pen, preferably one that you can photocopy without losing definition. If you do not have access to a computer, then why not ensure that your writing is on the large side and that your signature takes up as much of the page as is feasible. If your school or department does not already do so, try suggesting tick boxes for different subject skill areas. You could then add just one or two comments on the end of the report, rather than having to comment on the skills in full.

SOME USEFUL PHRASES FOR REPORTS

The following phrases should prove applicable to most subjects, as they give generalized comments about the sort of skills a student needs to succeed in their lessons, i.e. attitude, behaviour, concentration, etc. You will, of course, want to add your own subject-specific comments, for instance on factual knowledge, reading and writing skills, analytical ability, creativity, and so on. I have grouped the phrases into the categories given in the previous section which range from 'special problems' to 'really excellent' students. I have also provided some personalized comments that I might use as appropriate and a model report for each category of student. In this model report I omit any subject comments that you would, of course, need to include.

Students with special problems

Approach/attitude:
- Finds it very hard to take a positive approach to lessons.
- Needs to develop a more positive attitude towards this subject.

Behaviour:
- Has found great difficulty in maintaining suitable behaviour in class.
- Must ensure that he/she avoids disruptive or confrontational behaviour.

Concentration:
- It is essential that he/she develops his/her ability to concentrate for extended periods of time.

Co-operation:
- Must learn to co-operate with the other students in the class.
- Must ensure that he/she treats other students with respect at all times.

Communication skills:
- Needs to learn to communicate clearly and effectively.

- Must ensure that he/she listens carefully at all times.

Contributions to the class:
- Must learn to contribute constructively to the class.
- Should always value the contributions of other students.

Homework:
- Is having difficulty completing homework tasks on time.
- Must ensure that homework is completed to the best of his/her ability.

A model report

John has found it very hard to settle into this class. (*Personal comment which hints at, rather than states, the fact that John is a difficult and anti-social student.*) Although he does try his best, he finds it difficult to behave well. John must approach his lessons in a positive way and treat other students properly. If he is to make progress in this subject, he must learn to concentrate better. John must also complete all homework on time and as well as he can.

Weak students

Approach/attitude:
- Needs to develop a more consistent approach to this subject.
- Should aim to take a positive attitude to his/her lessons.

Behaviour:
- Should aim to behave in an appropriate manner at all times.
- Is working towards improving his/her behaviour in lessons.

Concentration:
- Is learning to maintain concentration for extended periods of time.
- Should concentrate fully on the tasks set.

Co-operation:
- Should be more willing to co-operate with all members of the class.
- Should treat other students with respect at all times.

Communication skills:
- Should aim to make more contributions to class discussions.
- Needs to listen more carefully to instructions.

Contributions to the class:
- Should aim to contribute his/her ideas on a more regular basis.
- Must listen carefully to the contributions of other students.

Homework:
- Should ensure that homework is completed to the best of his/her ability.
- Must hand all homework in on time.

A model report

Candice takes a positive approach to this subject but her enthusiasm can result in a lack of concentration. (*Personal comment which suggests that Candice is normally a good student but can lose focus at times.*) She finds some aspects of this subject difficult, but is trying hard to improve. Candice should ensure that she treats other students with respect at all times. She should also make sure that she completes all homework tasks set to the best of her ability. This will help her to develop in those areas of this subject which she finds hard.

Average students

Approach/attitude:
- Usually takes a positive approach to this subject.
- Has a positive attitude that he/she should aim to build on further.

Behaviour:
- Is generally well behaved during lessons.
- Is a quiet and polite student, who always behaves appropriately in class.

Concentration:
- Is working hard to develop his/her concentration.
- Should aim to concentrate for increasing periods of time.

Co-operation:
- Co-operates well with other members of the class.
- Is willing to work in a variety of different groups.

Communication skills:
- Offers some ideas to the class and should now aim to be more confident.
- Listens well to instructions.

Contributions to the class:
- Makes interesting contributions to class discussions.
- Listens well to what other students have to say.

Homework:
- Always hands his/her homework in on time.
- Completes all homework tasks set to a fair standard.

A model report

Fred is usually a hard-working student and he is always polite and well behaved in class. (*Personal comment which suggests that Fred is a fairly good student who behaves well, but could probably do better.*) He tries his best even when he finds the work difficult and always listens well to instructions. Fred should now aim to become more confident when contributing to class discussions and to complete all homework tasks set to the best of his ability.

Good students

Approach/attitude:
- Is a keen student who always takes a positive approach to lessons.
- Has an excellent attitude towards this subject.

Behaviour:
- Is always polite and well behaved in class.
- Sets a good example to other students by his/her behaviour.

Concentration:
- Can maintain a good level of concentration for extended periods.
- Shows good concentration when working individually.

Co-operation:
- Works very well with all the other students in the class.
- Is a co-operative student who always shows respect for others.

Communication skills:
- Always listens carefully to instructions.
- Offers some very interesting ideas in lessons.

Contributions to the class:
- Is always willing to make contributions to discussion work.
- Makes interesting and helpful contributions to the class.

Homework:
- Always completes homework tasks on time and to a high standard.
- Has produced some excellent homework assignments.

A model report

Kelly is a great asset to the class. She always approaches lessons in a positive way and shows a real talent for this subject. (*Personal comment that should please both Kelly and her parents/guardians. It is always encouraging for a student when a teacher suggests that they have a 'talent' for a subject.*) She has worked hard to improve her work and is a keen participant in lessons. She should now aim to become more confident about contributing her ideas to the class. It is a pleasure to teach such a hard-working student.

Excellent students

Approach/attitude:
- Is a keen and conscientious student who is always willing to participate.
- Maintains an excellent attitude in every lesson.

Behaviour:
- Has maintained his/her excellent standard of behaviour.
- Sets an excellent example for other students in the way he/she behaves.

Concentration:
- Can maintain excellent concentration for extended periods of time.
- Demonstrates a high level of concentration at all times.

Co-operation:
- Is always willing to co-operate and help other students.
- Shows excellent leadership skills during group work.

Communication skills:
- Communicates his/her ideas in a confident and eloquent way.
- Listens very carefully at all times and asks highly perceptive questions.

Contributions to the class:
- Has made some fascinating contributions to discussion work.
- Is a very valuable member of the class.

Homework:
- Is always beautifully presented with a high standard of content.
- Has completed some impressive homework assignments.

A model report

It is a pleasure to teach Jasdeep. He is an extremely conscientious student and he is producing work of an exceptionally high standard. (*Personal comment that suggests just how good Jasdeep is at this subject and also praises his approach.*) He sets an excellent example for other students in the way he behaves and he is always willing to co-operate with and help the other members of the class. His homework is always beautifully presented with an excellent standard of content. He should aim to continue working as he has been doing so far. Well done, Jasdeep!

Some personalized comments

- Is always polite and hard-working in class.
- Is a lively student with a very positive attitude.
- Is a very valuable member of the class.
- Shows a real talent for this subject.
- Is keen, conscientious and always willing to help.
- Has a very mature attitude.
- Is a real pleasure to teach.
- Is a talented student who should aim to fulfil his/her potential.

YOUR FIRST PARENTS' EVENING

One of the scariest experiences in your teaching career will be your first ever parents evening. As a student teacher, although you may have come into contact with parents or guardians, you will not have had to face them in such a formalized setting. Here are a few thoughts that may help you prepare for the nerve-racking occasion that is the parents' evening! Do bear in mind that after a few of these experiences you will wonder what you were ever scared about.

Appointments

In the run-up to the parents' evening you may be asked to book time slots for each parent or guardian. Do not worry too much about the accuracy of this. Inevitably, people are late or get delayed talking to other teachers and it is rare that you will actually stick to the appointment times. These appointment times do, however, help to give the students a sense that the parents' evening is an important event for them.

If you do not have many students, try to bunch the appointments together so that you don't have to wait for long periods of time. You could, if you wish, leave yourself free for the first half hour so that you have longer to relax after school. On the other hand, you may have a large number of classes (for instance if you teach a subject such as music or drama where you only see the students for one lesson a week). If this is the case I would recommend that you ask only those students whom you have concerns about to make an appointment. The others, if they really want to see you, should of course be given the opportunity.

Preparation

Do not try to make copious amounts of notes before the parents' evening. It is unlikely you will refer to them – it is better to be natural and talk to the parents or guardians about your own impressions of their child. If you feel it would help, have a few points written down that you would like to raise with them, perhaps a concern about homework, or a query about an extended period of absence.

Try to give yourself a break before the evening starts. You may find that there is half an hour to an hour between the end of school and the start of the parents evening. Make sure you have something to eat, as you may not finish until late. It is also a good idea to change your clothes, because you can bring a 'smart' outfit with you and also because you may feel rather 'creased' after a day's teaching. Looking business-like will help you feel ready to face the parents.

They are more scared ...

As with the first time your students meet you (see Chapter 1) you will find that some of the parents or guardians are more scared of you than you are of them. Keep this in mind and try to put them at ease. This will help you relax too. When they arrive, stand up and shake hands with them and identify which student they 'belong' to. If the student is with them, you have an added advantage, as you can praise (or embarrass) the student in front of their parents. If the student is there, a good starter question is: '*How do you think you've been getting on?*'

The discussion

Keep your discussion short and concise. There is no need to waffle on, as it will make you tired and will have little value. Comment on the student's work to date and give some ideas for targets that their parents or guardians may be able to help them with, for example, homework. If they have any specific queries that you are not sure about, make a brief note and say that you will talk to your head of department or a more senior teacher. Do ask the parents if they have any questions. They may well feel scared to ask you and this is also a good way of bringing the interview to an end.

Problems / problem parents

Although it is very unusual, you may find yourself in a situation where the parents or guardians become confrontational with you, perhaps criticizing the way you teach or the type of work you are setting. As an inexperienced teacher, this can be very difficult to deal with. If this does happen try to remain calm and rational, using the techniques discussed in Chapter 3 to defuse the situation. You could suggest arranging a meeting between you, the parents and your head of department at another time. In this way they can discuss their concerns in private and you will have the support of a more senior, experienced colleague to help you deal with them.

Missing

Inevitably, some parents or guardians will not turn up, either because they could not make it, or because they did not want to come (or because the student did not tell them that there was a parents' evening). Do try to check up on any students you are worried about. It is often the case that the parents you most want or need to talk to do not turn up. Your school may have a system whereby they do this for you, but if you do have strong concerns make a phone call home yourself (having told the appropriate pastoral manager that you are going to do so).

Part III

It's All About People

Chapter 9

Students

DIFFERENT TYPES OF STUDENT

It is likely that the majority of students you encounter will be well adjusted and keen to work. However, most teachers will also have to face students who have a problem or special educational need. As a professional, it is your duty to deal with these students in the best way that you possibly can, and to ensure that they have full access to a good education. You will also have to make sure that their behaviour does not jeopardize the education of the other students in your class, and this is often harder than it sounds.

When you collect your class lists you may receive information about those students with special educational needs. You will need to find out, preferably before you start teaching, just what the needs of the students in your groups are. Special educational needs are quantified by giving the students a 'level', going from 1 (lowest level of need) to 5 (highest). At Level 5 the student should have a 'Statement of Special Educational Needs' and such a student is sometimes referred to as a 'statemented' student. Details of the abbreviations commonly used for SEN are given in 'Identifying special educational needs' later in this chapter and in Chapter 12.

Try to avoid having preconceptions about your students based on the information you receive about their special needs. Students who have behavioural problems in some classes or subjects, or for certain teachers, may behave themselves perfectly for you. If you face the class having already made a decision that student X will be poorly behaved, you may find that your expectations create a self-fulfilling prophecy.

DIFFERENT TYPES OF GROUP

Different schools and subject areas use a variety of different methods for grouping their students, based on their intake and on their philosophy of education. Sometimes the tutor or registration groups in each year will contain students of mixed abilities, or the year group may be streamed. Stream A might contain students who are academically strong, while stream B could accommodate the weaker students. Each head of department or faculty will then take a decision about whether to set their students: they may decide to create top, middle and bottom sets; they may use only mixed ability groupings; or they could decide on a combination of both methods.

There is much discussion about whether students are better served by setting, streaming or by mixed ability teaching. You will come to your own conclusions about this, but in reality you will have little influence on the creation of groups until you gain promotion. I have based the following comments about teaching different sets purely on my own experience. They cover the advantages and disadvantages of different sets for you as a teacher, rather than from a philosophical perspective.

Teaching top sets

- *Advantages*   It is very enjoyable to teach a group of highly motivated and intelligent students. They stretch you intellectually and there are little or no discipline problems. You will move quickly through the work and you can try out some more creative strategies. There is usually little need to differentiate the work you set.
- *Disadvantages*   Bear in mind that your marking load will be heavy, as these students are likely to work at a fast pace. You will need to be on top of your subject in order to field any awkward questions. You may also encounter ambitious parents who question the quality or quantity of your teaching. Students in top sets can, on occasion, become arrogant or lazy because they feel that they 'know it all' already, and it is fairly difficult to decide how to discipline them for this behaviour.

Teaching mixed ability groups

- *Advantages*   There is a good mix of characters in a mixed ability group, and the stronger students may encourage the weaker ones to achieve better results. The students are generally fairly well motivated, but you will not have quite the marking load that you would have with a top set.
- *Disadvantages*   If there are disaffected students in a mixed ability group, they can affect the quality of the lesson for the more able or well-motivated students. This can cause tensions within the class between those who want to learn and those who do not. You will have to differentiate the work you set if there is a wide range of abilities in the class.

Teaching bottom sets

- *Advantages*   If you teach a bottom set your marking load is fairly small and you can keep well ahead of the students in terms of planning. Sometimes bottom sets are deliberately designed to contain a smaller number of students. You can use highly structured lessons and even try out some more unusual strategies that could appeal to these students. You may have support teachers or assistants to help you.
- *Disadvantages*   If the students have behavioural problems, there is the likelihood of some serious confrontations, especially if they are not willing to work hard and you

are pushing them to do so. With this type of group you are not intellectually stretched by the lessons you are teaching. You may find this type of group very tiring to work with.

ACCESSING RECORDS

It really is worth getting to know the people involved with SEN in your school as soon as possible (see Chapter 10). They can advise you on dealing with difficult students and will also fill you in on background information that helps you understand the causes of poor behaviour in your classes.

Ask to see the SEN records of the students you will be teaching (and tutoring) at the first possible opportunity. At the beginning of term all teachers are very busy and no one will show you these records unless you make a specific request. If you do this early on you will not have to find out about your problem students through bitter experience! You will also, hopefully, avoid saying or doing things that exacerbate any difficult situations. Again, though, I would stress that you should not prejudge your students on this material, merely use it to inform your style of teaching.

IDENTIFYING SPECIAL EDUCATIONAL NEEDS

The special needs teachers at your school will have a great deal of expertise in this complex area, and you should always refer to them for detailed information about the types of special needs your students have. There is also more information in Chapter 8 about the process of identifying students with special educational needs and how important it is for you to do this. There are many different types of special need, and I am certainly not an expert on the subject, but the more common types that you are likely to come across are as follows:

1. *Emotional and behavioural difficulties*   This is usually abbreviated to EBD and the term covers a wide range of problems. Students with these types of difficulties may exhibit confrontational behaviour, but equally they can be withdrawn or 'school refusers', i.e. those students who will not attend school. Bear in mind that, just because a student will not behave themselves in your lessons, they do not necessarily have a behavioural difficulty. Ask yourself honestly just how deep their problems go before you refer them to the special needs teachers. Talk to other members of staff to see whether they too have problems with the student.
2. *Specific learning difficulties*   Again, this term is abbreviated and students are described as having a SpLD. This term also covers a wide range of problems, but the problem is often only obvious in one particular area of the curriculum. An example of this would be a problem with spelling. If you see that one of your students is struggling with spelling, but is otherwise very strong academically, they could well have a specific learning difficulty.
3. *Dyslexia*   This term has become very popular, with parents as well as with teachers. It is often used (wrongly) to cover a multitude of problems with spelling, writing and so on. Do not throw this term around, using it to describe every student

who ever makes a spelling mistake. However, if you are interested in finding out more about the subject, there are many texts available. At the simplest level, the term describes a problem with recognizing words and this can range from mild to very severe.

4. *English as a second language / English as an additional language*   These two terms, abbreviated to ESL and EAL, basically describe those students who are not fully proficient in English. They could well speak another language at home and this may cause them difficulties in their lessons. A student whose first language is not English might have problems with grammatical constructions and also with technical terminology.

DEALING WITH PROBLEMS

How then, do you deal with specific problems that occur with students in your class? Look carefully at 'Setting the boundaries' in Chapter 3 before you start teaching. If your boundaries are clear, you will minimize poor misbehaviour. The case studies in the following section give detailed information on the options available to you, and the outcomes that you might expect, but here are a few brief tips for dealing with some of the more common behavioural problems:

1. *Isolate the troublemaker*   Every troublemaker wants an audience: after all, a lot of misbehaviour is really attention seeking. If you isolate the student, by taking them aside and talking quietly to them rather than getting into a confrontation in front of the whole class, you are denying them the 'oxygen of publicity'.
2. *Get down to their level*   It is much easier to reason with someone if you are *literally* on the same level as them. If the student is seated, crouch down beside them to chat to them. This immediately makes you seem more reasonable and lessens the authoritarian image that some teachers have which can lead to confrontations.
3. *Remain reasonable at all times*   It is very hard to be angry with someone who refuses to rise to the bait. If you remain calm and reasonable at all times, this should have a direct impact on a rude or confrontational student. Again, they will not receive the attention they are seeking. Perhaps, at home, the only way for such students to get a reaction from their parents or guardians is to become confrontational with them. The reaction they expect from you is probably for you to shout at them. If you refuse to do this, you will defuse the situation and start to train the student to trust you.
4. *Keep your voice quiet*   This calms the situation down and forces the student to slow down and consider their behaviour in a clearer way. Put yourself in their shoes and think about the difference between someone shouting back at you when you are angry, or staying calm. This tip will also stop you from becoming a loud teacher (see Chapters 3 and 4).
5. *Explain the problem*   Often, a student will not understand why or what they are doing wrong. Explain why their behaviour is inappropriate, ask them if they agree with you and if they understand what you are saying. By doing this, you are giving them a chance to address and change their antisocial or inappropriate behaviour.

6. *Stick to your guns* Back to those boundaries again! You are the teacher, you have set the rules and been fair and clear about it. Do not give in to a student in order to pacify them. If you do, you are storing up trouble for yourself in the future.

7. *State the sanction clearly* Staying calm and reasonable, inform the student of what will happen to them if they continue to misbehave. If the student (and the class) sees that you stick to your boundaries at all times, they will know the outcome of any misbehaviour.

8. *Depersonalize the sanction* Instead of making the student feel that he or she is receiving a personal reprimand, try to depersonalize the punishment you are going to give them by saying: '*If you continue to (state misbehaviour) I will have no option but to (state sanction).*' This helps to make you seem reasonable and fair.

CASE STUDIES

The following case studies are entirely fictitious and reflect a variety of the situations you may have to face. They give details about the student, what their problem is, and offer some ideas about how the teacher could deal with them. These are of course only examples, and much of how you deal with real-life problems depends on the situation you find yourself in, the type of class you have and the student's reactions to what you do and say.

The 'odd-one-out'

The student

Joe is rather a strange student. He lacks social skills and does not integrate well with the rest of the class. If you are honest, you can understand why they do not want to work with him. His behaviour is strange and he can become quite confrontational if the other students do not accept his ideas.

At the start of term, the students were willing to work with Joe, but as time goes on they are becoming increasingly frustrated by him and keep asking you not to make them work with him. You are becoming worried about what might happen if someone refuses point blank to co-operate.

Dealing with the problem

1. The first step to take is to find out, if you have not already, whether Joe is on the SEN list. If he is, you should ask for some more information about exactly what his problem is and what has caused it. If he is not officially recognized as having special needs, bring his problems to the attention of the appropriate person (see Chapter 10). He clearly has some sort of emotional or behavioural difficulty that needs to be addressed as soon as possible.

2. It certainly might be worth taking Joe to one side, perhaps after your lesson, and

discussing with him why he has trouble relating to the other students. You will need to be subtle about this, perhaps asking him if he feels he is settling in okay and if not, why not. You could also offer him some strategies to help him get on with the other students better, for instance, listening carefully to other people's ideas.

3.   At the start of the term you will, hopefully, have set the boundaries (see Chapter 3) and *all* the students must follow them. If any students refuse to work with Joe, simply state to them that they must respect the others in the class by working in the group you have put them in. Follow the appropriate sanctions if they refuse to do so.

4.   Another option is to 'fix' the groups to avoid any difficult combinations (see 'Creating groups' in Chapter 3). This avoids the possibility of confrontation, but these students (although they do not realize it) are influencing your teaching and you are not really addressing the root of the problem.

5.   If appropriate to your subject, or if you teach Joe PSE, you could do some work on making friends with the whole class in the hope that Joe will pick up some tips.

The potentially violent student

The student

Thelma is well known around the school for her violent temper, which seems to flare up out of the blue. She is usually a fairly well-motivated student and she has produced some good work for you. However, she does have a tendency to argue with a couple of other students in your group.

At the moment these arguments are only verbal, but they are getting increasingly vicious and you worry that they may flare up into physical violence. You can sense a lot of tension building up within the class.

Dealing with the problem

1.   Again, the first step is to check whether the SEN department knows that Thelma has a behavioural difficulty. If not, bring her to their attention. Ask for their advice on how you should deal with Thelma, as they may know about specific events or actions that make her temper flare up.

2.   Talk to Thelma individually about her behaviour, and try to help her work out what it is that makes her angry and how she might deal with it in an appropriate way. This may prove difficult if she also gets confrontational with you. Try to explain to her how other students and teachers feel about her behaviour rather than blaming her.

3.   Sit Thelma as far away as possible from those students she becomes confrontational with. If possible, sit her next to a well-behaved but placid student in your class. However, make sure that this student does not suffer because Thelma is sitting next to him or her. Another alternative would be to sit her at the front of the classroom so that she cannot see or talk to any other students. If she becomes

confrontational when asked to do this, explain to her that you are trying to help her control her temper by avoiding situations where it becomes a problem.
4. If Thelma does get into a confrontation, always try to defuse the situation by talking to her quietly, moving her away from the person she is quarrelling with, or by asking her to step outside to calm down (perhaps with a friend). If a violent confrontation takes place, you should try to encourage other students to intervene, rather than doing so yourself and laying yourself open to trouble. However, it is hard not to step in when a fight is actually taking place.

The student with poor concentration

The student

Fred generally behaves well in class, but he has a problem with finishing his work. His confidence in his work is very low and he rarely concentrates long enough to complete anything. He complains of tiredness if you ask him to write for more than five minutes at a time.

Fred's work is often very difficult to read and he has now started to distract other students near him by chatting to them when he runs out of steam. He very rarely completes his homework.

Dealing with the problem

1. Again, talk to the SEN department. It may be that Fred has a genuine problem concentrating because of a specific learning difficulty. This may also explain the poor presentation of his work – perhaps he is hiding the fact that he cannot spell or perhaps he does not understand the work you are doing.
2. Give him small but achievable targets when you are doing written work. For instance, put a line half-way down the page and ask him to aim to write down to that point by the end of the time given. Alternatively, you could ask him to aim to write as neatly as possible, rather than trying to complete the work.
3. Talk to him about why it is important for him to work neatly and complete the tasks you set. Ask him if there is a problem that you can help him with. At the same time, though, you must stick to the boundaries you have set for the class and sanction him for uncompleted homework and for chatting in lessons. Hopefully this will encourage him to concentrate.
4. It is possibly worth phoning Fred's parents or guardians to talk to them about his homework. This can often help a great deal by identifying the problem for them and showing the student that you care. They could spend time with him at home to help him complete his work.
5. He may find it helpful to work on a computer, as it is possibly the act of writing that is tiring him. If your school has a portable computer, you could ask to use it. Alternatively, you could use trips for the class to the computer room as a reward to encourage Fred.

The arrogant student

The student

Sandra is a very self-confident student in your top set class, but her confidence often comes across as arrogance. She completes all the work you set to a high standard, but she has started taking liberties with her behaviour in your lessons, talking while you are explaining the work and so on.

Sandra has started arriving late for your lessons. When you ask her where she has been, she always claims that the teacher in her previous lesson detained her, but never has a note to prove it. You believe she is lying to you. Whenever you try to challenge her about her behaviour, she says your lessons are boring and she doesn't enjoy them. She frequently says (loudly) that Mr Evans, the teacher they had for this subject last year, was much better than you. She also asks you repeatedly if you are a new teacher and others in the class are picking up on this.

Dealing with the problem

This type of student can be surprisingly hard to deal with, as they do not have a special educational need, but they can really disrupt your class without actually earning any sanctions. They can also severely undermine your self-confidence, especially if you are an inexperienced teacher.

1. Stick rigidly to your boundaries and if Sandra does overstep the mark, apply the appropriate sanction. For instance, explain to her that being late to class without a note means that she will receive a punishment, that you will impose on her just as you would on any other member of the class. Make sure that you are fair and that she receives the same treatment as everyone else. That way, she cannot complain.
2. It is very tempting, when a student says your lessons are boring, to respond in a negative way. You may not feel particularly confident about what you are teaching and this type of comment can be very hurtful. Fight against the temptation to throw a jibe back at Sandra: this is exactly what this type of student usually wants – attention. If she knows she is succeeding in hurting you then she will continue to do so. The best response (apart from ignoring her) is a bored 'Really, that's interesting.'
3. It is possibly worth talking to her about her behaviour and explaining why you feel it is unacceptable. Be aware, though, that in doing this you are acknowledging that she is getting to you. If she feels she has succeeded this may be just what she needs to step up her campaign. You could ask a more senior or experienced teacher to have a word with her (perhaps a head of department), but again you run the risk of undermining your authority.
4. Overall, the best response is to completely blank her anytime she says or does anything designed to attract your attention. If you get into a slanging match, she has won.

The unhappy or shy student

The student

Selina is a quiet, well-behaved student in the first year. She rarely puts her hand up in class, but she always completes her work quickly and neatly. In fact, the other students call her a 'boffin'. You have also heard them laughing at her glasses.

   She doesn't seem to have any friends in your class and you often see her wandering alone around the school at break and lunch-time. Recently she has become even more withdrawn in lessons.

Dealing with the problem

1. It seems possible, from the information here, that Selina is being bullied. The first approach is to talk to or write a note to her form tutor, rather than speaking directly to Selina, to see whether this is a possibility.
2. If you have built a strong relationship with Selina, then you could ask her what is wrong. Perhaps she came from a different school to all the other students and does not know anybody. You could mention that you have noticed that she is very quiet in class and ask her whether she wants to talk to you about anything. However, you do want to avoid making her feel even worse.
3. Try every way you can to improve Selina's self-confidence. Praise her work, preferably in written comments rather than in front of the class, to avoid the others developing this idea of her as a 'boffin'. You could also try to encourage her to become more of a participant in class discussions, but be wary of forcing her to answer questions.
4. Again, you could phone her parents or guardians, after consulting the appropriate pastoral manager. They might not realize that Selina is finding school so hard. It is probably best not to tell her that you have telephoned her home, as this could make her feel even worse.
5. Try to encourage the other students, perhaps ones you know are sensitive, to see if they can include her in break and lunch-time activities. You could also suggest that Selina joins a homework club or other activity that takes place during breaks, so she has somewhere to go and also so that she has the opportunity to make friends.

The verbally aggressive student

The student

Colin is an extremely difficult student and the SEN department have told you that he has severe emotional and behavioural difficulties. He claims that you pick on him and whenever you try to tell him off or ask him to complete work he reacts badly, throwing abuse at you. The standard of his written work is very poor and he rarely finishes anything.

Colin is also confrontational with the other students and none of them want to work with him. Your class has quite a few difficult students in it and you feel that Colin is dragging them down with him.

Dealing with the problem

1. Ask a special needs teacher to talk to you about Colin. If possible, try to find out the background to his problems so that you can avoid exacerbating them: perhaps it is something specific that sets him off. Ask for advice about how to deal with him and consider requesting a support teacher for your lessons.
2. Be as fair and firm as you can, sticking closely to the boundaries you have set and explaining why his behaviour warrants the sanction you give. Make it clear that, rather than the sanction being your choice, it is his choice because of the way he is behaving. At times you may need to bend your boundaries a little with this type of student, depending on how severe the problem is. You do not want to have to send the student out of every lesson, but they must understand that you will stick to your guns.
3. Use praise as much as you can – whenever you see Colin doing something even slightly well, commend him for it. It is very easy to slip into negative behaviour with a student like this, as you get very frustrated and the way that they treat you can be hurtful. Always keep in mind that this student has special problems and must have a very difficult life to behave like this: do not take what they say and do personally.
4. Try to get Colin working with some very good students, who will not respond to any disruptive behaviour and who will hopefully motivate him. Use careful praise of these students to encourage him to emulate them. Offer some really good rewards to the whole class and try to ensure that Colin wins one of them.
5. Again, it is probably worth telephoning or meeting the parents or guardians (perhaps before the parents' evening, if it is not early on in the year). A chat with them could shed light on why he behaves as he does, but do be careful about what you say.

Chapter 10

Teachers

GETTING TO KNOW THE RIGHT PEOPLE

Teaching attracts a range of people, some of whom will have started on their careers many years ago. A large secondary school may have as many as 100 teachers, working in various different departments. Your job will put you into daily contact with other members of staff, probably those in your department or in your pastoral team. However, there may be some teachers at your school who you would not meet in the course of your work, but that you should really get to know.

First, if you belong to a union, or are thinking of joining one, it really is worth getting to know any union representatives in your school as they can answer a variety of questions you may have. If it should ever be necessary for you to have a meeting with senior management, the union representatives can come along to this to act as a mediator or adviser and to ensure that you are treated fairly. For more information about teaching unions see 'Developing support systems' in Chapter 1.

It is also well worth being on speaking terms with the heads of the various departments in your school. If you decide to do any cross-curricular work, these teachers are a source of very useful information. It is also very helpful for you to get to know any experienced teachers who have been at the school for a long time, but who are not part of the senior management. Try to find someone you feel you could talk to if you have a query that may seem petty, but which is really worrying you.

Teachers sometimes overlook the office staff in a school, perhaps because they do not usually have much contact with them, and this is a shame. Office staff can make your life a lot easier, for instance if you have a letter you need typing, or information about a student, such as telephone numbers, addresses, etc. Take the time to get to know them: they perform a very valuable role in the running of the school and will generally be very happy to help you. If the headteacher has a secretary, try to get to know them as well. If you need fast access to the head or approval for something, for instance a trip, an amenable head's secretary can smooth your path.

Another important group of people involved in the running of the school, who again are often overlooked, are the buildings or caretaking staff. These might include a buildings manager, caretaker, cleaners, and so on. Again, it is very worthwhile being on speaking terms with these people. If, for instance, you need to book the hall or have some chairs moved at short notice, a good relationship with the buildings staff will smooth your way. The job of cleaning a school is a very difficult one, so think about how you might help the cleaners with their task. For instance, it might be helpful for your classes to put their chairs on the tables at the end of the day. You will certainly be assisting the cleaners if you ensure that your classroom floor is kept as clear of rubbish as possible.

Finally, as I have already mentioned, do get to know the teachers involved with special educational needs in your school. If you show an interest, they will have lots of valuable advice that they can give you about handling your more difficult students and they can probably offer you some specialized resources for your classes. You will also find it easier to gain access to student records if you are on speaking terms with these teachers. Again, their role is a crucial one in the smooth running of the school, and one that is perhaps underestimated at times.

GETTING TO KNOW THE WRONG PEOPLE

Unfortunately, there may also be some people in your school who you should avoid like the plague. These are the people who have stayed in teaching because they cannot (or cannot be bothered to) get another job. To them, teaching is not a vocation but an irritation. They will moan at every opportunity (and to anyone who will listen) about how dreadful the students are. Teaching is, of course, a tough job, and I would never try to deny that fact. However, the only way to give the students a fair deal (and to enjoy the job) is to work hard at it. Try as far as you can to avoid getting involved with this type of teacher.

TYPES OF TEACHERS

Here are some examples of types of teachers you may encounter and details about the way they might behave, inside and outside the classroom. These examples are, of course, entirely fictitious. I have made them rather stereotypical and, hopefully, fairly amusing. Teachers are individuals and use a mixture of styles in the classroom, depending as much on the class as on their own personality. However, you might like to see if you can recognize any of these types of teachers in your own school.

The 'old-school-tie' teacher

- *Dress code*   This type of teacher always dresses smartly and, if male, wears a suit and tie. They feel school uniform is vital for maintaining discipline among the students.
- *Favourite catchphrases*   The 'old-school-tie' teacher often uses sentences starting with '*In my day . . .*', for instance '*In my day children knew how to behave themselves.*' He or she also uses the question '*Would you do that at home?*' for various mis-demeanours, for instance if a student puts their feet up on a desk.

- *Discipline code* This teacher is a strict disciplinarian who believes that children or pupils (never students) should be seen and not heard.
- *Favourite method of discipline* This type of teacher would like to use the cane, but since they cannot, they will give their students a verbal thrashing instead. They are keen on giving out vast quantities of lines and lots of detentions. They also like to send students to stand outside the classroom, where they immediately forget about them until the inspectors or the headteacher arrive, at which point they instantly become a model teacher.
- *Teaching style* There is a strong focus on traditional methods and working in silence in this teacher's lessons. There will be little exploratory or creative work.
- *Marking strategy* This type of teacher uses a red pen to put lots of crosses, a few ticks, and a mark out of ten on each piece of work.
- *Bad habits* The 'old-school-tie' teacher has a tendency to turn red and spit when he or she gets angry, which is rather frequently. The male of the species has a poor taste in ties. Irritatingly for you, they like moaning out loud (but not to anyone in particular) in the staff room.
- *Classroom layout* The desks are invariably in rows, facing the teacher.
- *Condition of desk* Their own desk will be very neat, with only one pile of marking to be done and lots of red pens to use when doing it. Do not, whatever you do, borrow a pen or move any of their papers.
- *Advantages* The students will know where they stand with this type of teacher and will probably be well disciplined, although unfortunately this is often through fear rather than respect. He or she will usually achieve good results with able, well-motivated students.
- *Disadvantages* Quiet students are often too scared to answer questions in this teacher's lessons and there is little opportunity for group work. Weaker students may exhibit bad behaviour as an excuse to escape from the classroom.
- *Marks /10* Educational value = 7
  Development of creativity and imagination = 2
  Quality of discipline = 7
  Equality of opportunity = 2
  Scale of student appreciation = 2
- *Total score /50* 20

'The students are my mates' teacher

- *Dress code* This teacher dresses in a casual style, often wearing trendy labels. He or she tries to dress like the students to get 'in' with them. They are not keen on the idea of school uniform and tend to overlook minor infringements of the rules.
- *Favourite catchphrases* Again, this teacher tries to emulate the students, '*Check it out*' is a current favourite. If a fight between two students starts, they will try '*C'mon, let's be reasonable about this guys.*'
- *Discipline code* They base their discipline code on the theory that, if you let the students do what they want, they are likely to work harder. This type of teacher feels comfortable with lots of noise and activity.
- *Favourite method of discipline* He or she believes that: '*The students will discipline*

themselves if they feel sufficiently motivated and any misdemeanours are an expression of the students' frustration at an outmoded schooling system, which denies young people a sense of identity and seeks to destroy their natural creativity.'

- *Teaching style*   There will be a great deal of exploration and issues-based work, usually in groups. This teacher avoids traditional methods such as 'chalk and talk'.
- *Marking strategy*   This teacher only gives positive comments and feels that using red ink will demotivate the students. They are also strongly against the concept of a right or wrong answer, even in fact-based subjects.
- *Bad habits*   Among this teacher's bad habits are: talking while the class are chatting; using too much jargon when talking to other teachers; and drinking alcohol and smoking (sometimes *with* the students!).
- *Classroom layout*   Desks are usually set out in groups, but sometimes he or she likes to get rid of the furniture altogether and have an impromptu 'drama session'. There will generally be much movement of desks, often in *your* classroom. They are unlikely to return the furniture to its original position.
- *State of desk*   Their desk is neat, but only because all their papers are in one pile. At the bottom of the pile is that really urgent report that this teacher should have completed three weeks ago.
- *Advantages*   The students will probably like this type of teacher, partly because they will feel relaxed, but also because they will be able to get away with murder. This teaching style encourages creativity and individuality.
- *Disadvantages*   Unless the students have a natural sense of discipline, chaos will probably reign. The class will be very noisy and this may trouble students who would prefer to concentrate on their work.
- *Marks /10*   *Educational value = 7*
  Development of creativity and imagination = 10
  Quality of discipline = 3
  Equality of opportunity = 6
  Scale of student appreciation = 7
- *Total score /50*   33

The ultra-efficient teacher

- *Dress code*   The ultra-efficient teacher always dresses smartly: if male he wears a suit and tie, if female she wears a smart jacket, often with a skirt. He or she feels that school uniform is important and will impose the school rules on a fair and consistent basis.
- *Favourite catchphrases*   *'I'd like you all to face the front, make eye contact and listen carefully.'*
- *Discipline code*   The ultra-efficient teacher has a strong sense of discipline, but is not necessarily seen as strict by the students. This type of teacher believes that everyone has an equal right to a good education and will impose the discipline necessary to achieve this.
- *Favourite method of discipline*   He or she will apply any school behaviour code to the letter and will contact the home if they feel a student is consistently misbehaving.

- *Teaching style* The lessons will be very clear and well organized with a good balance between teacher- and student-led sessions.
- *Marking strategy* This teacher combines written comments on the work with close marking of errors.
- *Bad habits* This teacher's bad habits include a refusal to see the worst in any student and a tendency to cosy up to senior management because of their ambition to get promotion quickly. Irritatingly, for mere mortals, their reports are always beautifully presented and handed in on time, or even before the deadline.
- *Classroom layout* The desks are usually set out in rows, facing the teacher, but the ultra-efficient teacher sometimes moves the furniture for group work and will always return it to its previous position.
- *State of desk* Their own desk is neat, with lesson plans for each day carefully laid out in advance. Photocopied resources for the next three weeks will be ready for use.
- *Advantages* The students know where they stand and will respond well to a teacher who applies consistent standards. Their work will be neatly presented and all students will be given equality of opportunity.
- *Disadvantages* Creativity is sometimes stifled, but this is not always the case. This type of teacher can be rather depressing for other members of staff, as they feel that they could never be so efficient.
- *Marks /10* Educational value = 9
  Development of creativity and imagination = 7
  Quality of discipline = 9
  Equality of opportunity = 9
  Scale of student appreciation = 7
- *Total score /50* 41

The joker

- *Dress code* The joker wears fairly casual, usually 'fun' clothes, for instance brightly coloured ties and T-shirts with amusing captions on them. They couldn't care less about school uniform.
- *Favourite catchphrases* The joker starts most lessons by saying: '*Do you want to hear a joke?*' In fact, this is their favourite question to the students and to the staff. The joke will invariably be rude.
- *Discipline code* This type of teacher feels that if the students find the lessons funny, they will behave themselves. Surprisingly, this actually often works.
- *Favourite method of discipline* The joker disciplines classes by making fun of any student who misbehaves. Joke punishments include the student standing in the corner with their hands on their head.
- *Teaching style* This teacher uses lots of anecdotes from his or her life to illustrate the subject being taught. For instance, geography work on polluted rivers may consist of a story about the time the joker and his or her friends got drunk and threw a shopping trolley into the local river. A lot of lesson time is spent with the students listening to the teacher talking and telling jokes, during which he or she likes to jump up on the desks to add variety.

- *Marking strategy*   The students' books will be full of jokey comments that he or she is perfectly happy for them to respond to.
- *Bad habits*   See 'favourite catchphrases' (telling bad jokes) and 'dress code' (wearing bad ties). The joker also tends to get rather strange haircuts.
- *Classroom layout*   The desks are set out in rows, facing the teacher, not because of any particular educational philosophy, but so that all the students can hear the jokes properly and see any accompanying demonstrations.
- *State of desk*   The joker is not renowned for his or her tidiness. They will probably have a drawer full of handy practical jokes to play on teachers and students.
- *Advantages*   The students tend to respond well to this type of teacher. A lot of the time school can be very boring, so it is good for them to have a laugh. They will also (hopefully) respect the joker.
- *Disadvantages*   Not a lot of subject teaching goes on because the joker spends so much time telling his or her jokes. The quiet students tend to just sit there while the louder ones will join in and probably get more attention.
- *Marks /10*   Educational value = 6
  Development of creativity and imagination = 9
  Quality of discipline = 7
  Equality of opportunity = 6
  Scale of student appreciation = 9
- *Total score /50*   37

The chaos theory teacher

- *Dress code*   This type of teacher looks as if their outfit was thrown together in a force ten hurricane in about ten seconds that morning. Their hair looks slept on and has not seen a comb in recent history.
- *Favourite catchphrases*   This teacher is usually spotted wandering around the staff room asking, '*Has anybody got a red pen I can borrow?*' As exam time draws near, this will change to: '*I'm sure I had that set of really important GCSE exam papers a minute ago ... now where did I put them?*'
- *Discipline code*   What discipline code? Chaos rules here and the students must sink or swim. Some of the students are quite happy sitting at the back of the room on the floor smoking a cigarette.
- *Favourite method of discipline*   This type of teacher believes that having a chat to the offenders to try and discover what makes them tick will work miracles.
- *Teaching style*   The chaos theory teacher practises what is known as 'discovery learning'. This translates as 'the kids do what they like and hopefully a little bit of learning takes place, probably incidentally'. He or she may be a real expert on their subject, but can have trouble putting the information across.
- *Marking strategy*   Their marking strategy is straightforward and works every time: just lose the books before you have to mark them.
- *Bad habits*   Disgustingly, this teacher has a habit of absent-mindedly picking their nose or scratching their bottom. For other bad habits see also 'marking strategy' (losing books) and 'dress code' (incredibly messy).
- *Classroom layout*   The desks are usually set out in rows, to impose a little bit of

order on the class. However, by the end of the lesson the rows are disbanded altogether (by the students, rather than by the teacher) and the desks positioned so that friends can sit together.

- *State of desk*   Their desk looks as if the proverbial bomb has hit it. This is in fact probably one of the main reasons for this teacher's marking strategy: somewhere beneath the debris are those vital exam papers and all those lost exercise books!
- *Advantages*   They are usually a real expert on their subject and the students will respond well to this. Their teaching style can also lead to some very creative ideas.
- *Disadvantages*   The bright kids may do well, but the less able tend to get lost in the whirlwind that this teacher lives in.
- *Marks /10*   Educational value = 7
  Development of creativity and imagination = 8
  Quality of discipline = 2
  Equality of opportunity = 4
  Scale of student appreciation = 7
- *Total score /50*   28

The earth mother or father

- *Dress code*   If female, this teacher wears a long pinafore dress, sometimes made of corduroy, and flat shoes with her hair tied back in a bun. If male, you can spot him by his 'Jesus' sandals (worn, in impeccable style, with socks) and his long beard.
- *Favourite catchphrases*   'Now then, children, let's all settle down and do some work, shall we?' is used by this teacher as the class start to riot. Students are called 'children' by the earth mother or father up to the age of about 15.
- *Discipline code*   This type of teacher tries to encourage self-discipline in his or her children, as they feel that it is wrong for teachers to be too disciplinarian. He or she asks quietly for silence and is usually noisily ignored.
- *Favourite method of discipline*   The earth mother or father believes in talking to the children about why they did what they did and why they shouldn't do it again.
- *Teaching style*   Their style is soft and gently spoken. The lessons tend to consist of talking to the class for a while then asking them to explore a topic. This teacher rarely raises his or her voice, except when they begin to panic as they realize the class is rioting and the head is coming down the corridor.
- *Marking strategy*   In a nutshell, this teacher's marking strategy involves positive comments only, and no red pen or crosses allowed.
- *Bad habits*   His or her bad habits include talking while the children are talking, not washing their hair very frequently, and wearing socks with sandals.
- *Classroom layout*   The desks are set out in groups, so that the children can 'share their ideas'. There are lots of environmentally friendly posters on the walls.
- *State of desk*   The earth mother or father has a neat desk, with lots of little personal items, such as a cuddly toy, a photo of his or her family, and so on.
- *Advantages*   This type of teacher is usually good for quiet and weak students, as they will receive lots of personal attention and a gentle, caring approach.
- *Disadvantages*   There may be poor classroom control, the lessons do not stretch the more able students, and those with behavioural difficulties may take advantage.

- *Marks /10*   Educational value = 7
                Development of creativity and imagination = 7
                Quality of discipline = 6
                Equality of opportunity = 6
                Scale of student appreciation = 7
- *Total score /50*   33

DEALING WITH SENIOR MANAGEMENT

It is likely that you will have very little reason to deal directly with senior management. The first person you turn to when you have problems will usually be your mentor, the head of your department, or a head of year or other pastoral manager (if the problems are with your registration group). If you choose to apply for promotion, you will have increasing contact with them as you progress, but at this stage in your career you will not usually have any reason to approach them.

It is always worth having senior members of staff on your side, as they can assist you if you have any major problems or if you need approval, for instance of a trip or of time off. Members of the senior management of a school are 'on duty' at all times, so remember this when you are dealing with them. Be careful what you say – you may believe that you are making a joke, but they might take what you see as humorous comments in the wrong way. Finally, bear in mind just who it is that decides promotions in a school.

Chapter 11

Parents

I use the term 'parents' throughout this chapter to describe whoever takes care of the student at home. There is a wide variety of different types of family unit and a wide range of people who will care for the students. The term 'parents' is used to include all of these: from single parent families, to guardians such as foster parents, grandparents, brothers and sisters and so on.

DEVELOPING THE TEACHER–PARENT RELATIONSHIP

If you use the analogy between a school and a business, the parents of a student are the clients of the business. Of course, unless you are working at a private school, the parents will not be paying directly for your 'services', but indirectly, through taxation. However, they are still entitled to know (and will demand) that the service offered by your school, and by you individually as a teacher, matches their expectations. As in any business, it is important to develop a good relationship with the people that you are working for. This is especially important in education, of course, because the parents can back up the work that you do in school with their children at home.

There are various ways that schools try to develop the relationship between teachers and parents. I give some ideas for communicating with parents in the next section. There are also some thoughts about using parents as a resource in Chapter 4: this is certainly a worthwhile way of developing the parent and teacher relationship as it has benefits for you, your students and their parents. Another idea is to ask your students to bring in information gathered at home from their family, for instance, details of a family tree for a history project or statistics about the size of their family for mathematics work. You could also ask your students to tape a conversation with their parents, perhaps for use in a project about the local area or about where the different students come from.

Schools will usually have a parent-teacher group, the Parent–Teacher Association (PTA), that aims to strengthen the links between home and school. This group will also have a role in raising funds for the school. If you have the time or inclination, it can be useful to become involved with the PTA. You may also find that you want to request some of the funds they raise for a project in your own department.

COMMUNICATING WITH PARENTS

In a secondary school the main form of communication with parents is usually through any formal reports and at the parents' evenings. Reports offer a good form of communication with the home, although they have their limitations. The report is often a rather one-way process, the teacher informing the parents rather than having a dialogue with them. In some schools, though, the parents or students are asked to give a response to the report. The parents' evening offers a better chance to communicate, although again this is only a brief encounter and in reality offers little opportunity for extensive conversation. Chapter 8 covers reports and parents' evenings in more detail.

One of the best ways to communicate directly with parents is by telephoning them. Before doing this, do check with the appropriate manager that it is acceptable. Telephoning parents is especially effective if a student is not completing homework, or has missed time at school without a valid reason (this, of course, comes under the role of the form tutor). You should be able to find the relevant telephone number in the register or by asking the office staff for assistance. If you talk directly to a parent in this way, you will usually find them more than willing to back you up. The students also seem remarkably impressed by the fact that you have phoned home – I would suggest this is partly because you have taken an interest, and partly because most students genuinely care about what their parents think of them.

Most schools (and many departments) will have a variety of standard letters that you can send home, for instance if coursework is missing. This will save you the time spent in making a telephone call, particularly if you have difficulty getting through. However, sending a letter does lack the directness of speaking to a parent on the phone.

TYPES OF PARENT

You will come across a variety of parents in your teaching career: the majority being genuinely supportive people who want to help you succeed in teaching their child. A minority of parents, unfortunately, will be less helpful and some may even prove very difficult to deal with. You should remember at all times that, as discussed previously in this chapter, the parents are the clients and you are the one providing a service: always stay calm and polite when you are speaking to parents, however much they antagonize you. A good way to avoid confrontation is to use some of the tactics you would employ with a difficult student (see 'Dealing with problems' in Chapter 9).

I would like to offer you a few brief ideas about how to deal with some different types of parents, although obviously each parent (and each child) is an individual. The way you deal with parents will vary a great deal according to the situation you find yourself in and also the policies of your school and department. The best advice is to concentrate on doing your job as well as you can, and not to worry too much if you do have the occasional conflict.

Supportive parents

Supportive parents are a delight to work with: they believe that you know your job, but they are there to back you up should you ever need it. They encourage their child to do the best they can and to take the work (and homework) you set seriously. If possible, try to involve this type of parent as much as you can with the school, for instance asking them to visit your class to give a talk or to help individual students with their work.

Overambitious parents

It is very difficult to deal with this type of parent. They want the best for their child, but unfortunately their ambitions sometimes outstrip what their child is capable of, or what the student wants for themselves. These parents can make life difficult for the teacher as well, asking why you have set particular work and suggesting that you don't know how to do your job. The best policy with this type of parent is probably to humour them as much as possible, but not to alter what you have decided to teach because of them.

Overprotective parents

Some parents worry a great deal about how their child is settling into the school, and because of this probably have a rather negative impact on the child. You should try to answer their worries, particularly if you are the child's tutor, but keep reassuring them that you will look out for their child and contact them if there are any serious problems.

Parents who abdicate responsibility

This type of parent believes that the child is the school's problem, and that you should deal with any difficulties that come up. They believe that their responsibility ends when the child leaves the home. Again, it is hard to deal with this type of parent, but bear in mind that the child may well see school in a rather negative way and will probably need lots of praise and encouragement.

Potentially abusive parents

If you suspect that a student is being abused at home, either physically or psycho-logically, you should notify the special needs teachers and the appropriate pastoral manager or deputy head at once. They may be aware of the situation, but you would not be doing your job (and you would be failing the child) if you did not make your concerns known. It is not your responsibility to deal with such serious problems and you do not have the specialist knowledge required to do so. Pass your concerns on, in writing, immediately.

DEALING WITH COMPLAINTS

From time to time, parents will complain, either about what you are teaching or about how you are teaching. You will know whether these complaints are justified, and for the most part they will not be, but unfortunately they really are just part of the job. Stick to your guns – if the work you have set is in line with departmental and school policies, if the sanctions you have given are fair and the student has earned them, then you are acting professionally as a teacher. Be confident in yourself: even though you have only just started teaching, you are a professional and have undertaken the appropriate training for your job.

If a parent complains directly to you, perhaps over the telephone or by letter, you should talk to a more experienced member of staff before responding. Your mentor, pastoral manager or head of department will have more experience in dealing with parents and can help you decide what to do. Explain the situation as clearly as you can, stating exactly what you have done and why. Your colleagues should be more than willing to back you up. If the parent complains indirectly, perhaps to your head of department, find out exactly what they said and again make your position clear. Do not worry too much. As I have said, these complaints really are unavoidable, even for the best and most experienced teachers in a school.

PARENTS AND EXAM RESULTS

Some parents will have unrealistic expectations of the way their child is going to perform in exams. Similarly, some students will not perform in the way you expected, perhaps through nerves or lack of preparation. In the run-up to the examination year the parents and students will usually have plenty of warning about what the exam results are going to be – mock exams, comments on reports, discussions at parents' evening and so on. If the student does underperform, or you feel that the exam results may be incorrect, it is well worth speaking to your head of department. Exam papers can be re-marked, and students can resit exams. Again, trust your professional judgement: if the student has underachieved even though you did your best for them, you have discharged your responsibility and you should not worry.

Part IV

Just Part of the Job

Chapter 12

The Language of Teaching

TACKLING TERMINOLOGY

When I started working as a teacher I was surprised to find out just how widespread the use of 'technical' terminology and mystifying abbreviations was in the profession. Of course, there is sometimes a need to use these terms. However, they also help to give a degree of mystique and inaccessibility to the profession. They can be used to distance the non-specialist and make you (us) seem cleverer and more academic than perhaps we are. The same applies to technical terminology used within subjects. Try to remember at all times that you are serving the students and their parents or guardians, particularly when you come to write reports. If there is no need to use a complex or technical term, then choose the simpler and more accessible version every time.

ABBREVIATED TERMINOLOGY

The use of abbreviations is widespread in teaching and has its advantages and its disadvantages. One of the main advantages of using abbreviated terminology is that you will save yourself time in both writing and speaking. Obviously, if OFSTED are coming to visit your school, you do not want to say 'the Office for Standards in Education' each time you mention the subject. Similarly, when writing things down, it is easier to put SATs than Statutory Assessment Tests each time.

However, the time-saving aspect of abbreviations does have its negative side. A number of these terms are connected to the special needs work in schools, and these can create a strong tendency to label the students. '*He's got EBD*,' a teacher will say, as if the student has a disease. He does not, of course, have 'EBD'. He has a particular emotional or behavioural difficulty, for instance an inability to concentrate or to control his temper. Another problem with abbreviations is that for the new teacher they can be very confusing at first.

A BRIEF GUIDE TO ABBREVIATED TERMINOLOGY

Many of these terms will be in daily use at your school, and after a while you will find yourself using them with ease. Please bear in mind that they will vary from school to school and from area to area.

A level	Advanced level – post-GCSE qualifications taken by sixth formers.
ADD	Attention deficit disorder – a new term that describes extreme concentration problems.
AR&R	Assessment, recording and reporting marking, reports, parents' evenings and so on.
BT	Beginning teacher – a new teacher. This term seems to change regularly.
CDG	Curriculum development group – a working party (see other terms) to discuss the curriculum.
EAL	English as an additional language – English is not the only language.
EBD	Emotional or behavioural difficulty – a type of special educational need.
ESL	English as a second language – a student for whom English is not the first language.
GCSE	General Certificate of Secondary Education – exams taken at the end of Key Stage 4 (see below). This combines what used to be called the O (ordinary) level and the CSE (Certificate of Secondary Education).
IEP	Individual education plan – specific targets drawn up for an individual student with SEN.
INSET	In-service training – courses and other training for working teachers.
KS	Key Stage – Key Stages 1 and 2 are primary and middle school. Key Stages 3 and 4 take students up to GCSE.
NQT	Newly qualified teacher – the old version of beginning teacher.
OFSTED	The Office for Standards in Education – the current term for school inspections (see Chapter 16).
PDG	Pupil development group – a working party that discusses issues involving the students.
PSE	Personal and social education – teaching students how to be 'whole' people.
PTA	Parent–Teacher Association – a parent and teacher group that raises money for the school.
SATs	Statutory Assessment Tests – exams at the end of Key Stages 1 to 3.
SEN	Special educational needs – a student who has a special educational requirement.
SMT	Senior management team – usually the head and deputy head(s).
SpLD	Specific learning difficulty – a problem with learning in one particular area (see Chapter 9).

OTHER TERMINOLOGY

As well as abbreviations, you will also come across a range of terms that may seem puzzling at first, but will become clear with time. Here is a brief selection:

Colleagues	The latest politically correct term for other staff at your

	school.
Development plan	Your school and your department will have short- and long-term plans that detail the developments that are going to take place. These are required by the inspectors and set out short- and long-term targets for a school.
Professional development	Any courses you might go on, or other forms of education that will develop you professionally. Professional development would also cover opportunities for promotion.
Statement	In full, a 'Statement of Special Educational Needs'. A student who has a 'statement' will be experiencing considerable problems in their education. At this level, educational psychologists and other professionals will be involved in working with the student.
Working party	A group that meets to discuss school developments. You may well be invited to take part. See Chapter 13 for comments on this.

Chapter 13

Meetings

THE STAFF MEETING

Generally speaking there are two kinds of staff meeting: the regular briefing-type meeting which is fairly short and deals with the day-to-day practicalities of running a school; and the formalized meeting of all the staff that will take place approximately once a term. The main features of each type of meeting differ quite substantially.

The staff briefing

Depending on the school you are teaching at, there may be a staff briefing once a day, once or twice a week, or perhaps on a less regular basis. This type of meeting allows the different staff within the school to communicate important information quickly and easily to each other. In a large school this is a useful way of informing all the staff at once of an upcoming event or a particular problem with a student.

This type of meeting will usually be far less formal than the staff meeting and there will probably not be an agenda. The briefing may be opened by the the head or deputy head(s) giving information to the staff, for instance about promotions or expulsions. The other members of staff may then be invited to raise any points they wish to make.

There are certain members of staff who will normally need to speak at this briefing: the pastoral managers (heads of house or year) could give updates on particular students, for instance if someone in their year or house group has been suspended; heads of department may give information about trips or forthcoming events in their subject area, and so on. If you have anything you need the entire staff to know urgently, this is the forum at which to do it: it can however be very nerve-racking to talk to a staff room full of people!

The formal staff meeting

Formal staff meetings are part of your directed time – the statutory hours that a teacher must work – as opposed to the actual (voluntary) hours you might put in. These formal staff meetings are usually timetabled well in advance on the school calendar. They will normally take place after school (probably in the staff room or another room big enough to take all the staff) and may go on for up to two hours. In most cases, though, they would be about an hour long. The head may publish an agenda the week before the meeting takes place and put it in your pigeon-hole or on a staff noticeboard.

Often the head and deputy head(s) do most of the speaking at these meetings and they will cover whole-school issues, such as development plans or inspection visits. Depending on the size of your school, you may be required to contribute, or merely to soak up the information that is being given. These meetings may also be given over to group work where you are required to discuss an issue in a smaller group and then report your ideas back to the whole staff.

THE DEPARTMENT MEETING

It is likely that you will also have regular department meetings (perhaps once a fortnight), at which you discuss subject-specific issues. These may take place before or after school, or perhaps in a lunch-time or free period when everyone in the department is available. In a large department, these meetings are an important means of communicating information between different teachers. If run well, departmental meetings are a valuable source of updating and will also give you the chance to mix more regularly with the other members of your department.

At these meetings, members of the department will usually share information: details of syllabus requirements, upcoming exams, schemes of work, visits, and so on. If someone in your department attends a working party at the school, for instance on whole-school assessment policies, they might have information to disseminate. Your head of department could also decide to use some of your meeting time to moderate work, for instance for GCSE coursework, or plan termly or yearly schemes.

THE MEETINGS TRAP

As well as these 'statutory' meetings, there will be many other meetings going on after school. Your presence will not be required at most of these, as attendance is often limited to staff in positions of responsibility. However, there will also be other working parties that meet perhaps once per half-term.

At the start of the year, each department may be asked to put forward staff to sit on these working parties. Depending on the way your school is set up and run, these meetings are either a complete waste of time, or a very valuable chance to contribute to what happens in the school. As with extra-curricular activities, it can be valuable to be able to say you were on a working party when you apply for other jobs, as it shows you are willing to get involved in every aspect of the way your school is run. Similarly, you may value the chance to meet staff from other departments or areas of the school, and you may have some excellent ideas (or a specialism) of your own that you would like to develop.

Do not feel pressurized into joining these working parties unless you are sure you have the time. No one will mind if an inexperienced teacher does not volunteer to help out, but you could find that others take advantage of you because you are fresh, uncynical and keen to offer your services. If you can guarantee that you will only have to attend a couple of meetings a term, and do no other work, then it may be worth your while volunteering. However, beware of the 'meetings trap' whereby you end up doing lots of additional paperwork, writing plans, disseminating information to your department, and so on. If you are already involved with a lot of extra-curricular activities, for instance if you teach sport, drama or music, you will have a very good 'get-out clause'.

Chapter 14

Extra-curricular Activities

WHY GET INVOLVED?

People often associate extra-curricular activities with teachers of particular subjects, for instance drama teachers (the school play), music teachers (the school choir and orchestra) and PE teachers (football, netball teams, and so on). However, there is no real reason why this should be so and it is still worth becoming involved with this aspect of the school if you possibly can, even if you do not see yourself as a specialist. Not only will the students get to see an entirely different side of you, but you will also find these activities satisfying and useful for your curriculum vitae (CV). There are, however, various considerations for the inexperienced teacher to bear in mind, particularly the fact that you do not want to overstretch yourself and neglect your 'real' teaching.

THE ADVANTAGES

Foremost among the advantages of taking part in extra-curricular activities is the opportunity to get to know the students in a more relaxed environment. You will also meet students who are not in your classes, ones you would not normally teach or talk to. Unless you teach in a very small school, it is probable that you will only encounter a fraction of the school population at any one time. When you do meet these students as a teacher, perhaps a year or two later, they will already have had good experiences with you and are likely to feel much more positive about you. It may also surprise you to discover that students considered difficult in academic subjects become completely different during extra-curricular activities. Many of them will have talents in areas you had never suspected and it is always rewarding for both student and teacher to see success and achievement taking place.

Taking part in extra-curricular activities shows a real willingness to get involved in the life of your school, beyond your compulsory teaching duties. When you move to another school you can demonstrate on your CV that you are an enthusiastic and energetic teacher. You will also have a wider variety of experiences to talk about and you will have developed a range of skills. For instance, if you did the lighting for your school play, you will have extended (or found) technical skills that could enhance your teaching. You will also have shown the ability to work as a member of a team, an ability not normally particularly strongly developed in teachers, whose job by its very nature is a solo activity.

In addition to the opportunity of developing better relationships with your students, you will also get to know a wider range of other teachers in a climate that is likely to lead to friendship, or at least to mutual supportiveness. Finally, you will find personal satisfaction from taking part in extra-curricular activities. You can stretch and extend yourself, perhaps into areas that you were previously unsure about or in which you lacked confidence.

THE DISADVANTAGES

There are, of course, some negative aspects to getting involved with activities after school. The most important of these is the time consideration: how much time can you afford to take away from your planning, marking and administrative loads? If, for instance, you get involved with a school football team, you could find yourself working late after school perhaps two or three nights a week. You may also want to accompany your team to matches and these may take place on a Saturday or Sunday morning. A commitment to extra-curricular activities means giving up your own free time.

Once you start getting involved after school, extra-curricular activities have a tendency to escalate. The other staff and the school management see that you are willing, and perhaps try to push you into becoming overinvolved and taking on more responsibility than you should. On the other hand, the management at your school may feel that inexperienced teachers should be concentrating on developing their classroom practice, and may actively discourage you from involvement.

SOME TIPS ON TRIPS

In my experience, one of the most memorable school experiences for many students is the chance to go on a trip. For some, they may never otherwise have this opportunity, perhaps because of money considerations. Trips can seem like a great adventure for students in which they get out of school and see a little of the real world. Of course, trips also have a very valid educational justification behind them. For the teacher, too, a trip is the chance to be out of school for a day (or more) and get to know the students better in a different environment. So, if you are approached to take part in a trip, for instance a visit to a museum, an art gallery or the theatre, say 'yes' immediately.

There is no reason why a relatively inexperienced teacher should not organize a trip. However, I would caution you to follow your school trips policy to the letter and perhaps also find a more experienced colleague who is willing to support and assist you. There are legal obligations involved with taking students out of school and it is very important that you are aware of these. You are *in loco parentis* – in the role of a parent – and if there are any problems you are legally responsible. However, as long as you are careful and follow the 'school rules' to the letter, you will find organizing a trip a very worthwhile experience.

The normal requirement for a staff to student ratio would be around one adult for every ten students. If you are taking a large group try to find a range of teachers from different subject areas to accompany them. This will give the students the benefit of a wider range of personalities and will also allow you to get to know some more of the school staff in a more relaxed environment.

Before you go you will need to send letters home, asking for permission, and also for a voluntary contribution towards the costs. You will have to collect return slips and money, which can prove to be an administrative nightmare, so make sure you leave sufficient time before the trip to do this. Many schools have a budget set aside to help students who cannot afford the cost of trips and you should check how this works before you start. You should also find out where and how to pay in the money you receive. In reality, you may well find that you have to use your own money (or credit card) in order initially to finance the trip. This fact, along with all the organizational difficulties, is what puts many teachers off organizing and making trips.

If the trip is by coach, you will need to find a suitable company. Ask other staff for advice – geography teachers will often have this information because they have to organize field trips. If the trip is taking place outside of normal school hours, you should arrange a meeting-place for your students. At the end of the trip this could be where you will 'drop them off', although you should remain with them until they have all been collected. The students may become very excited during the trip: it is your duty to calm them down and ensure that they behave themselves. Normally, however, this is not a problem, as they will be enjoying their day out and will not want to jeopardize it with poor behaviour.

Finally, bear in mind that organizing trips is also an excellent experience to have on your CV when you apply for jobs. It shows initiative, and also (as with any extra-curricular activity) a willingness to really become involved with your school. If you do not have the opportunity (or confidence) to organize your own trip, try to get invited on one of the trips organized by other members of staff. The advantages of doing so are the same as with extra-curricular activities: and sometimes a day out of school can be just what you need.

Part V

Testing Times

Chapter 15

Mentoring and Appraisal

THE ROLE OF YOUR MENTOR

If you are assigned a mentor (see Chapter 1) he or she will play a vital role when you start teaching: your mentor is the person you turn to if you have any questions or problems and they will probably be responsible for watching some of your lessons to evaluate your progress. They should also ensure that you are not taking on too much on top of your lesson preparation and marking. If you are lucky enough to have a good and supportive mentor, this will make your life much easier.

You should have regular meetings with your mentor, in which they set you targets and help you assess your own progress, dealing with any worries that you may have. A little way into your first term, you should discuss your first formal evaluation. Hopefully, your mentor will allow you to choose a class for them to watch. It is not necessarily beneficial to choose an 'easy' class: it may be better to prove to them (and to yourself) that you can deal with more difficult or challenging students.

GETTING THE MOST FROM YOUR MENTOR

As a new teacher, you may feel at a disadvantage in the relationship between you and your mentor, who will have more (perhaps much more) experience than you. Do bear in mind, though, that your mentor will have volunteered for the role and will usually be very keen for you to do well. Find out when your mentor is available to sit and talk to you, rather than catching them at break when they may have other things on their mind. It is a good idea to set a specific time each week when you can meet for a discussion. Let them know what other responsibilities you have taken on, both to show how willing you are, and also to show them what your workload is like. They should be able to advise you about whether these extra activities are a good idea.

Ask your mentor early on about what the mentoring process involves: how many meetings and lesson evaluations you should expect, how much detail they will want to see in your lesson planning and longer-term schemes of work. If the class that they are going to evaluate is a difficult one, be honest with them and tell them about any problems you have had. It is more impressive for them to see you trying (and succeeding) with a class you find difficult, than watching you teach a class that requires little skill to control. Having said this, do not get them to watch the proverbial 'nightmare' class, at least in the first term.

PREPARING FOR APPRAISAL

Even experienced teachers are required to undergo regular appraisal and this type of 'testing' should be seen as an important and useful part of your job. Appraisers take different approaches when they evaluate a class: some like to get involved, moving around to question the students, to look at their books (and check your marking) and to help anyone who needs it; others may simply sit in a corner at the back of the room and watch what goes on from there. You could, of course, ask your appraiser if they will assist you in a particular part of your lesson. This would demonstrate initiative on your part and, if your appraiser happens to be a teacher in your subject area, they could be a valuable resource for you.

When you (or your appraiser) have chosen a lesson for evaluation, you should prepare carefully for this formalized review. Generally speaking, this is a very worthwhile process and one that you should get used to. It is almost certain that, at some point in your teaching career, you will have to face an official inspection (see Chapter 16). You will, of course, have faced appraisal by your tutors many times during your training at college. Indeed, recent graduates are perhaps better prepared for this process than those who have been in teaching for a long time.

There are some things that you should do to ensure that you stand the best chance of receiving a good report. Many of the tips given in Part I of this book will come in handy when you are being appraised. You might find it useful to reread the sections on preparing for your first lessons and controlling your classes, particularly the 'Ten tried and tested tips'. You will have many things on your mind when you are being appraised, but it is important for you to demonstrate just how good a classroom teacher you really are.

1. *Show your appraiser the lesson plan* Your appraiser will probably ask to see a copy of your lesson plan beforehand but, if they do not, you can demonstrate how organized you are by doing so. They may also be able to give you advice, for instance, if they feel that you will not be showing a sufficiently wide range of skills for them to evaluate, or if they feel you are aiming to do too much in the lesson time available.
2. *Use a mixture of approaches* Your appraiser wants to see that you are utilizing a variety of methods in your teaching: for instance the teacher giving instructions, the students taking part in discussions, doing individual work, and so on. More ideas about this are given in Chapter 2 in 'Balanced lesson planning'. They also want to see the students engaged in a variety of activities, although you should avoid the temptation to have too many different things going on at once as this could create discipline problems.
3. *Be well prepared* If you are planning to use any equipment, for instance a video clip to illustrate a subject you are covering, do ensure well beforehand that it is

available and working. If you are going to need materials such as paper, pens, paints or photocopies, there is nothing worse than having to scrabble around five minutes before the lesson trying to sort them out. Similarly, if you are planning a practical demonstration, it is probably worth going through it once beforehand to ensure that you know exactly what you are doing.

4. *Use interesting resources*   Lots of ideas about finding interesting resources are given in Chapter 4. It is always worth being inventive with the resources you use, as the students will respond more positively and your appraiser will hopefully be impressed and interested in your ideas.

5. *Stick to what you know*   Now is not the time to try something completely new with your class – you will confuse the students and you may well 'throw' them into misbehaviour. They will be aware that something different is going on, and may comment on it, which could be rather embarrassing for you.

6. *Take care with timing*   Your appraiser will watch the opening and ending of your lesson particularly closely, as one of the most obvious signs of a well-prepared and organized teacher is how they manage these times. Make sure you have an orderly start and finish. Remember that you may get caught up in your teaching and not notice that time is running out, so keep a close eye on the clock.

7. *Demonstrate your classroom management skills*   You should aim to impress your appraiser not only by good subject content, but also by how well you can control the students. In the run-up to your evaluation, refer the class back to the boundaries you set at the beginning of term, particularly if it has been a while since you last discussed them.

8. *Remain positive*   It is very tempting, when you are under the stress of being 'tested', to react negatively to any students who do play up. Stick closely to the boundaries you have set and give out sanctions (and rewards) firmly and fairly, just as you have been doing. If you look as if you mean business, and if they have built up respect for you, the class will work with you and for you.

9. *Warn the class*   This is a matter of individual taste: should you warn the class that someone will be watching them, or just wait and see how they react when your appraiser turns up? If you do warn them in advance, just say something like: '*Mrs Johnson will be coming to watch our class on Thursday to see what we're doing and how we're getting on.*' Do not tell them directly that it is you who are being appraised, although some of them will probably work this out for themselves.

10. *Marking*   Do ensure that your marking is fully up to date. However, do not alter your marking policy just because your appraiser is going to be looking at the books. The students will soon pipe up: '*Miss, you never normally mark our books like this!*'

11. *Relax*   Above all, remember you are only just starting out as a teacher – you don't have to be perfect yet. No one will realistically expect you to have mastered every aspect of being a teacher, otherwise there would be no point in appraisal. Even the most experienced teachers can have an 'off' day. Remember that your appraiser is a teacher too – they will understand!

FEEDBACK

After the appraisal, make sure you get the feedback you are entitled to, as soon as possible. Teachers are all busy people, but there is no point in being appraised if you do not find out what you did right or wrong and why. You will probably receive both verbal feedback and a formalized written evaluation, which may take a little time to prepare. Once you have heard what your appraiser has to say, discuss your own opinions with them. They will want to see that you can evaluate your own teaching. As suggested in Chapter 1 one of the best ways for you to improve and progress is by learning to see what went wrong or right in your own lessons, and why.

Your appraiser should also set you some targets to work towards for your next evaluation. There should be no more than about three of these, and they should cover the problem areas that they feel you need to work on. You should receive a copy of your formal written evaluation and the school will put another copy on your personnel file. Your appraiser will probably ask you to read the evaluation and to sign it to show that you have had the opportunity to discuss it.

Chapter 16

Surviving Inspection

PREPARING FOR AN INSPECTION

So, how unlucky do you have to be for your school to receive an inspection when you have only just started teaching? Statistically, the chances must be quite slim, but it is by no means an impossibility. The longer you stay at any school, the more chance there is that the inspectors will pay a visit sooner or later. The 'failing' schools and 'failing' teachers that the inspectors root·out receive a great deal of publicity, but, on the other hand, all the successful and thriving schools seem to get very little.

Even if you are at a school that you believe is going to do badly in its inspection, remember that as an inexperienced teacher you will have very little responsibility. As long as you are doing your job to the best of your ability, and consistently striving to improve your teaching, there is very little for you to worry about. If you came into teaching straight from college, all the latest developments in the profession will be fresh in your memory. You may also be more enthusiastic and have more energy than the teachers who have been in the profession for a longer time.

Your school will receive warning that it is going to receive an inspection well in advance. Indeed, they will probably know (and tell you) at your interview if an inspection is coming up. This advance warning has its good and bad points. It gives the school plenty of time to prepare, to get documentation in place, to help the weaker teachers improve (and perhaps exclude some of the more difficult students). However, it also leads to a climate of expectation in which rumours abound about the horrors of inspection.

THE MYTHS ABOUT INSPECTION

As the arrival of the inspectors gets closer and closer, the myths will start to multiply and take on a life of their own. The senior managers at your school will, of course, be under a lot of stress at this time. They may warn you that everything you say will be taken down and used in evidence against the school; that the inspectors will be particularly concerned with your subject; that every lesson plan and department handbook will be closely scrutinized.

It is possible that you will have to use a particular format to prepare your lesson plans and your department may work itself into a frenzy, getting handbooks and schemes of work in place for the inspection (handbooks and schemes of work that will probably never see the light of day again after the inspectors have gone). You will be warned that, if the inspectors come to see you and don't like what they see, they will keep returning again and again to your classes. The myth will probably circulate that you are sacked on the spot if you 'fail' (i.e. if you receive a bad score for a particular lesson).

THE REALITY OF AN INSPECTION

In reality, it is likely that observations of your lessons will happen no more than three times in the week of inspection. In many schools there are relatively few inspectors to go around and some inspectors will cover more than one subject. In an inspection at my previous school, when we reached Thursday of the inspection week and I still had not been 'seen', my head of department had to *request* that someone observed one of my lessons so that the inspectors could see the practice going on in our department. This situation may, of course, vary in a smaller school. However, even if you are 'seen' by the inspectors on several occasions, this does not mean that they have found anything wrong with your teaching.

When an inspector arrives in your lesson they will probably ask for a copy of the lesson plan and you should have this easily to hand. If they do not ask for your lesson plan, hand it over anyway. After all, you have spent all that time preparing for your moment of glory and you should show the inspectors exactly what you are capable of. Irritatingly, this means that you will have to have detailed plans ready for every lesson that you are due to teach that week. However, the amount of information required is not great. It is fairly unlikely that the inspector, with a full timetable of classes to watch, will be able to stay for the entire length of the lesson. It is of course likely that they will leave just as the best bit of your lesson begins!

The scores of each teacher are given to the head and it is his or her choice whether or not to share them with you: even if you do receive the top mark, you may never be told. One of the sad facts about school inspections is the missed opportunity: most teachers *want* to know what others think they are doing right or wrong. If you have received a low or even a fail mark, there are provisions in place whereby the school must work with you to improve your teaching. There is *no* truth in the myth that you will get sacked.

INSPECTION AND THE NEW TEACHER

As a new teacher you will have absolutely no curriculum responsibility and will only be responsible for ensuring that you teach your own classes properly. This means that if a secondary school department is disorganized, it will not be you that comes under fire.

The head of your department has full responsibility for ensuring that all documentation is correct and in place: schemes of work, handbooks, and so on. If an inspector does come to watch your lessons, they will know that you are an inexperienced teacher and they should take this fact into account.

Part VI

Onwards and Upwards

Chapter 17

Professional Development and Promotion

COURSES

Your training as a teacher does not end once you qualify and it is likely, particularly if your school has access to a good training budget, that you will get the chance to go on courses. Take every opportunity offered to do so: not only will you be developing and updating your knowledge about teaching, but you will also have a day, or days, out of school. It is also important for your CV that you can show an interest in maintaining your subject knowledge and extending your skills. Going on a course gives you the chance to refresh yourself, both personally and professionally. Courses for teachers are commonly known as in-service training (INSET).

If you are academically minded, if you are seeking promotion to the highest level, or if you would like to move into further education, it is useful to do a postgraduate qualification, such as an MA. It is sometimes possible to do this part time with the assistance of your school (both financially and with your timetable). Unfortunately, this situation is becoming rarer as schools and local authorities are forced to make budget cuts and savings. You may also find that you do not have the time or energy to go to evening classes when you first start teaching.

AIMING FOR PROMOTION?

At some point in your teaching career, you will need to decide just how far you would like to advance. In my experience, promotions in teaching rely on a number of factors, not just how good you are at your job. Being in the right place at the right time when a post becomes available is often an important element in gaining promotion. Because of the limited movement available within any one school, both in terms of the jobs available and also the fact that teachers have a tendency to stay where they are, you may simply find that no promotion opportunities occur. In this case you will have to think carefully about whether you want or need to move to another school to find promotion.

As you get promoted, your actual teaching timetable will generally become lighter and lighter. For instance, a head of department in a secondary school may only teach 18 hours a week, while the 'normal' teacher has 21 hours. A head of year may only have a timetable of 15 hours a week to allow them time to do their job effectively: meeting parents, attending case conferences, and so on. You need to decide at a fairly early stage whether you want to spend less and less time in the classroom. If your eventual aim is to become a deputy head or head of a school, be aware that you will find yourself spending very little time actually teaching, and far more on management and administrative tasks.

There is quite a lot of pressure in teaching to aim for promotion, but do bear in mind that there is no compulsion to do so. Some teachers dedicate their careers to becoming the best teacher that they can: they do not want to leave the classroom or take on any management responsibilities, they find more satisfaction in committing themselves to their students. Of course, one of the reasons many teachers aim for promotion is financial: as a 'standard' teacher you will reach the ceiling of the pay scale after seven years. (Chapter 18 explains the way the pay scale works in more detail.) The 'points' that come with promotion will boost your salary, although never by a substantial amount. Even the head of a large secondary school will only be earning a fraction of what he or she could get in a commensurate position in industry.

If you do decide to aim for promotion, there are generally two types of promoted position in a secondary school: pastoral and curriculum. A pastoral role involves looking after the students' needs and welfare in the school as a whole, while a curriculum role includes teaching and managing a specific subject (or a group of subjects in a faculty).

TYPES OF PROMOTION

Table 17.1 demonstrates the most likely route for promotion in a secondary school and the points that could be given for each job (although these are subject to a lot of variation). Clearly there are many pathways to the different posts available, for instance a head of year may move across to a head of department post if they have sufficient subject experience.

Table 17.1 *Promotion in a secondary school*

Pastoral	Curriculum
Deputy head of year/house - 1 point	Key Stage 3/4 co-ordinator – 2 points – often only English, maths and science.
Head of year/house – 2–4 points	Deputy head of department – 2–3 points
Deputy head – depends on the size and type of school	Head of department – 3–5 points – depending on the subject and size of department.
Headteacher – depends on the size and type of school	Head of faculty – 4–5 points – often a senior teacher.

THE ADVANTAGES OF PROMOTION

As mentioned before, one of the main and most obvious attractions of taking a promotion is the resulting increase in salary you can expect. However, there are clearly other benefits, as the salary increase is not exactly enormous. As you are promoted, you will have more and more responsibility: responsibility for increasing numbers of students and for managing other members of staff. This additional responsibility can lead to increased job satisfaction and you will also have the chance to make more of an impact on the policies and philosophies that your school uses. This decision-making aspect of the job increases the higher you go up the scale, with the head having overall responsibility for determining how they run their school (with reference to the school governors, local authority and government requirements).

If you become a head of department or faculty, you can influence and indeed dictate the procedures used within your area. You are also in a position to develop the role of your subject within the school. You will be employing, managing, developing and promoting other teachers within your area and this can be very rewarding. You will have your own budget to manage for buying books, resources, and so on.

As you go up the scale of status within any school, you will receive a degree of instant respect from the students. This is obviously qualified by how they see you as a teacher, but students are going to give more (or more instant) respect to their head of year than to a 'normal' teacher. Behaviour in your classes may therefore improve as a result of promotion, although this is by no means automatic.

THE DISADVANTAGES OF PROMOTION

Over recent years, teachers have been asked to play more and more of a managerial role in schools. Despite being trained to work in the classroom, they often have to do a completely different job, requiring very different skills. As you move up the promotion ladder, be aware that this will happen to you. You will have to manage teachers as well as students, both jobs that are very difficult and highly stressful. You will have to manage a budget, which is not easy if you have no financial experience. In a pastoral role, you will move further and further away from your subject, perhaps one of the main motivating factors for a career in teaching. Once started on the pastoral route, it can be difficult to move back across to promotions in your own subject.

As a manager you are likely to spend a lot of time dealing with the more difficult students, whose problems (and the problems they create for their teachers) you must try to solve. You will also have to interact with parents or guardians, again often the parents of the problem students. One of the joys of teaching is interaction with bright, well-motivated students, and this will lessen as you move up the scale in favour of disciplining those who have done something wrong.

Taking on a role with more status will also require you to adopt a different persona to that of the classroom teacher. A 'normal' teacher can, after a few years' experience, adopt a more relaxed style with their students. This is not really an option if you are a pastoral manager or deputy head. You will have to be 'in role' at all times, dressing and behaving appropriately. As a head of year or house you will probably have to run assemblies for a large group of students and this can be a rather frightening prospect.

As you advance up the scale of responsibility you will have to attend a wide range of after-school meetings and this will take up much of your free time at the end of each day. The increased administrative workload that comes with promotion may mean that you also have to sacrifice involvement in extra-curricular activities (see Chapter 14). If you have to attend three meetings a week because of your role of responsibility, it will be very difficult for you to be involved with the school play, for instance. Finally, the higher up the scale you go, the more likely it is that 'the buck stops with you' if anything does go wrong.

Chapter 18

Salaries and Pensions

HOW THE SALARY SCALE WORKS

Let's face it, you didn't come into teaching for the money, or if you did I'd advise you to take a serious look at your career choice right now. The money will never be brilliant, even if you make it right to the top of the pay scale as a head in a large secondary school. However, teachers do have the advantage of a standardized pay scale that gives them guaranteed pay increases up to a certain point. With promotion comes more money, although how much more will depend a great deal on the way your school is run. Chapter 17 gives more details about promotions.

The teaching salary scale can seem rather confusing at first, but the points listed below set out the basic details for teachers working in the United Kingdom. Many of the salary points are available for allocation by your school or local authority rather than paid to you on a statutory basis. This means that, if your school wishes to save money, they may choose to award you the lowest salary that they can. They may also offer you a one-year contract, renewable depending on how you perform. If you join a union (see Chapter 1) you will receive detailed information on the latest pay rates and how the scale works. You union can also advise you about the acceptability of a fixed-term contract.

1. *New teachers*   As a good honours graduate (1st, 2.1 or 2.2) you will automatically receive two points, so you will start on spine point two. If you are a graduate of any other type, you will start on point zero.
2. *New teachers with other experience*   There are quite a few points available here (up to nine), but much will depend on how your school views your experience. It will, of course, be far cheaper for them to give you only one or two points for additional experience.
3. *Yearly increases*   With each full year of experience, you will automatically be awarded an extra point, up to spine point nine. So, a standard good honours graduate will, after seven years in teaching, reach the top of the salary scale (unless they receive a promotion).

4. *Promotions*   On top of the points you receive for teaching experience, promotion points offer you additional money, up to five extra points. Chapter 17 gives more detail about the points that go with promotion.
5. *Special needs*   Two points are available for teachers in special schools or those who have special responsibilities in mainstream schools.
6. *Recruitment/retention/excellence*   Although points are available in these categories, it is rare to ever see them given. Schools often claim that such points are divisive between the staff but a cynic might also point out that they cost a school money.
7. *London weighting*   Statutory supplements are given to teachers in inner and outer London to account for the higher costs of living and working there.
8. *Deputies/heads*   A different scale applies once you move up into these positions and much is dependent on the size and type of school.

PROMOTIONS: MONEY FOR NOTHING?

After your first year in teaching, you may feel tempted to go for a promotion of some sort. As you advance up the scale, it is true that your teaching workload actually decreases, and by the time you reach the position of head or deputy head you would only be teaching a few classes a week (if any). However, with these positions comes much additional responsibility that cannot really be quantified in terms of hours of work. There is a lot more information in Chapter 17 about the advantages and disadvantages of taking promotion. However, do bear in mind that the higher up the scale you go, the more time 'in role' you will spend: a headteacher is always a headteacher, with all the responsibilities that entails, whereas a classroom teacher can more easily 'switch off' when not in school.

WHY NEW TEACHERS ARE POPULAR

Inexperienced teachers are 'cheap' for any school as they are right at the bottom of the pay scale. An increasing emphasis on financial management in schools is perhaps leading to the devaluation of experienced teachers, who cost a school much more in financial terms. New teachers are usually willing and have lots of energy, whereas after a few years of teaching you may well feel exhausted and cynicism could start to creep in. One final reason new teachers are popular is those one-year or fixed-term contracts: a school can far more easily find a reason to offer a new teacher a single year in which to prove themselves.

TEACHING PENSIONS

When you are young a pension is the last thing on your mind: '*Why bother?*' you might ask yourself, '*I can always do that later.*' With teaching, there are some excellent reasons for joining the pension scheme. The first is that it is one of the real perks of the job, offering a very good return on the money invested. Second, you may find that you wish to take early retirement and there are (at the moment) some provisions for this although, unfortunately, these are rapidly being whittled away. I would therefore advise you strongly not to opt out of the teachers' pension scheme. If you would like to find out more about pensions, or wish to make additional contributions on top of the standard ones, ask your union representative or finance department who can give you the name and contact number of a pensions adviser.

Chapter 19

Moving On

THE RIGHT SCHOOL?

After your first year or two, you should have a fair idea about whether the school that you are working in is the right school for you. However, it is important to differentiate between the inevitable tiredness associated with the end of the year and the need to find a new school (or career). There is absolutely no point in going through the work associated with looking for another teaching job (you remember it – the endless form filling and letters of application) if you are going to be moving from the proverbial frying pan into the fire.

You could look around your local area to see if there are any schools that interest you, and perhaps ask to make visits to some of them, particularly if there are jobs available. Remember, there is a lot more to choosing a school than just the quality of its students. Remember also that no school is perfect: what you need to decide is whether the good points about your school outweigh the bad. Moving after only one or two years at a school is a big decision to make – especially as you will just be becoming familiar with the way things work.

Think also about how long you want to stay in one place: I believe that one of the biggest problems with the teaching profession is the temptation to stay at the same school for a long time – after a while, it simply becomes easier not to move. You know the students, the staff, the systems, you may have gained promotion within your department, but is it necessarily beneficial for you or for the school to stay for those reasons? In order to help you decide whether you need to move or not, think about how your school scores in each of the following areas.

Management

Are the managers (head, deputy head(s), heads of department, pastoral managers) at your school approachable and willing to support and develop their teachers or have they lost touch with what it means to be in a classroom? How many hours a week does the head of your school teach? If he or she sits in an office, handing down commands from above without ever experiencing the students in the classroom environment, perhaps they are out of touch with teaching and teachers.

Staff

Do the staff at your school relate well to each and support each other's ideas and work or have they become cynical and lazy, either through disillusionment with the job or with the school? Do they socialize outside school and, if they do, do they talk about the school in a positive or negative way? Do the different departments within your school work together or in isolation? One of the signs of a good secondary school is a lot of interaction between the various different subject areas.

Another consideration is how well you get on with the staff at your school: they do not have to be the centre of your social life, but you will be spending a lot of time working alongside them. Do you have at least a few things in common?

Support systems

Think about who you can turn to if you have a problem. In theory it should be your line manager, but does this work in reality? A good school should support and develop its new (and existing) staff, so consider how supportive your school has been to you as a new or relatively inexperienced teacher. Would you say that the staff in your school support each other outside work? Think about who supports the students in your school when they have problems and whether their problems are dealt with properly or 'swept under the carpet'. Consider also who supports any teachers with problems and how this is done: for instance, does 'staff development' really consist of persuading old (and expensive) staff to leave?

Your department

In secondary schools heads of departments are increasingly asked to become managers, and some of them are just not cut out for this role. Ask yourself how well your head of department suits this role and whether you believe it is important for him or her to fulfil this managerial part of the job. For instance, if some members of the department are not 'pulling their weight', will your head of department clamp down on them or just ignore the problem? Of course, some heads of department are excellent despite not being managers as such, so consider also whether you are gaining valuable insights and experience from yours. Another consideration is whether you are getting the opportunities you need within your department or school, both in terms of teaching (A level, top sets, a wide range of classes and so on) and also in terms of promotion.

The students

Do the students at your school show respect for each other, for their teachers and for their environment, and is there a good mix of students who all get along with each other? It can be very wearing to work in a school where there is difficult behaviour, but this is also a challenge that you may miss if you move to that grammar school in Surrey. Think carefully about what you want out of teaching. Single sex schools or 'good' schools may be easier to teach in, but the increased load in marking and preparation can make up for the lack of behaviour problems. Above all, do you find the students interesting and challenging to teach? This is what you must spend most of your day doing, so think long and hard about this one.

The curriculum

Is your school innovative in the way it approaches the curriculum and are the managers up to date with the latest thoughts, ideas and innovations? Think, too, about the way your school organizes the curriculum: does your subject get as much priority as you would like or as you think it deserves? How are the subjects divided: are there faculties where several subjects are grouped together, or do the departments remain very much divided?

Administration, paperwork and meetings

Consider whether your school makes every effort to ensure that it keeps these time-consuming aspects of the job to a minimum. When you come to write reports, do you (and other teachers) consider them a vital and informative method of communicating with the students' home, or are they an ineffective use of your time? When you attend meetings, do you find that they are efficiently run, interesting and a valuable part of school life?

Buildings and facilities

The place in which you work will have a significant impact on you, both in terms of how and what you teach, and also the way that you and the students regard the school itself. If there is a lot of graffiti and the buildings are all very run down with a lack of facilities, it can have a real impact on the way the students behave. Think about whether the room or rooms you teach in are adequate for you and, if you have any complaints about your environment, whether they are taken seriously and dealt with quickly or not.

Promotion prospects

If you are looking for promotion, you may need to move schools to find it, depending on what is currently available at your school. Ask yourself whether your managers consider your 'professional development' important. There is far more information on this aspect in Chapter 17.

Extra-curricular activities

Are there a variety of well-supported extra-curricular activities at your school? This is usually, although not always, a sign of a good school as it indicates that both the staff and the students are keen and well motivated. If there are extra-curricular activities, do a variety of staff get involved, or is the job of running them left to just a couple of departments?

HOW TO GET GOOD REFERENCES

There is (what I hope is) an 'urban myth' in teaching about references: that if the head of a school wants or needs to get rid of a teacher, they will write them an excellent reference in order to 'help them move on'. Teaching is rather a peculiar profession in many ways, not least of which is the fact that teaching interviews are long and convoluted, but often do not actually require you to prove that you can do the one thing you are being employed for, that is to teach!

When you apply for your next job the school will usually ask for two referees, probably your head and your head of department or line manager. If you are efficient and get on well with them, you should have no problem getting good references. Make sure they have a list of all those 'extras' you have been involved with (see Chapter 14). Do warn your referees that you have applied for a new job *before* they receive a request for references: it is only polite and will improve the chances of your receiving a good reference. Try to make sure that they also have an idea of the type of job you are applying for, so that they can adapt their reference to suit it.

APPLYING FOR JOBS

As the year passes, you will take part in many different aspects of school life, so do make sure that you keep a note of all the 'little extras' that you contribute to your school. There is nothing worse than coming to write the letter of application for your next job, only to realize that you cannot remember which working parties you were on, how many plays or concerts you helped with, and so on. Write *everything* down as you go along. Schools want to know that you are an enthusiastic teacher who likes to get involved with all aspects of the life of the school. You should demonstrate in your letter of application how you have done this at your current school.

Even if you are not desperate to move, bear in mind that if you do get an interview for a job it will be good experience for you (and will get you a day out of school). Going for an interview will also demonstrate to your managers that you are looking for further development in your career. If you are an asset to the teaching staff at your school, they may decide that they do not want to lose you, and consequently try to offer you some sort of internal promotion or development. Be realistic about the jobs that you apply for – there is not usually much point in applying for a job which is more than two points above yours in terms of salary, but this is not always the case. There is more information on promotions in Chapter 17.

IS TEACHING THE JOB FOR YOU?

After training for a specific qualification, there is a real temptation to remain with teaching, even if you are not sure that it is the right job for you. At the end of your first year or two you will have gained some experience and can make a more rational judgement about your choice of career. Do bear in mind, however, that teaching becomes easier the more experienced you become – the first year or two is always hard, no matter how talented a teacher you are.

Think very carefully (during your lovely, long summer holidays) if you are having doubts about teaching. Perhaps have a chat with an experienced member of staff who you can trust to be discreet. Remember also that you may just be in the wrong school or teaching the wrong type of students for you (see 'The right school?' in this chapter). The following lists some of the plus and minus points of a teaching career and may be helpful to you in deciding whether teaching is the career for you.

The rewards

- You are your own boss – to a large extent you teach what you want.
- You are working with the subject that you enjoy, day after day.
- There is good job security and pay rises are automatic.
- The job is as creative as you want to make it.
- The job is as big as you want to make it.
- You can make a *real* difference to your students.
- You can form lasting relationships with students and staff.
- If you are good, your students will always remember you.
- There is excellent variety from day to day.
- You can gain valuable experience of a variety of roles and situations.
- The actual school day is very short.
- It is a good job to combine with having a family.
- The teachers' pension is a good perk (see Chapter 18).
- The holidays really are very good indeed – this is a *big* perk.

The negative aspects

- The job is physically and emotionally tiring.
- The job expands to meet the extent of your dedication.
- You will encounter difficult and even disturbed students (and parents).
- You may be put at risk of injury from these students.
- The nature of the job can lead to cynicism.
- The salary will never be brilliant and only rises very slowly.
- Your friends in other jobs will rapidly start earning (a lot) more.
- There is a lack of genuine promotion prospects for many teachers.
- Ironically, experienced teachers become too expensive for some schools.
- You will often have to work late, in your own time, to do a good job.
- You may be too tired to appreciate those lovely long holidays.

LEAVING

So, you have made the decision to go, and now the moment has come. You have told all your different classes and been faced with reactions from '*Great!*' to '*Please, Miss/Sir, don't leave*'. Leaving really is a double-edged sword – on the one hand you will find out how your students actually feel about you (hopefully good), on the other hand you will be leaving behind colleagues and students that you genuinely care about, having worked with them very closely for a long time. You may also feel guilty about leaving some classes half-way through a course. Don't – if you use this as a reason not to leave, you will never get out of your first school.

On your last day you will hopefully receive lots of cards and presents. In many ways, Christmas is a good time to leave a school, as everyone is on a 'high' anyway and there will be lots of parties going on. You may have to give a leaving speech, but do remember one thing before you list all the grievances you have about the school or the head – you might need a reference from him or her in the future!

Finally, I would like to wish you luck in the future, wherever and whatever you teach. As I said at the start of this book, you have made a wonderful choice of career. Try to look on the difficult times as a challenge and enjoy those indescribable moments of joy when you make a new discovery with a class, help a weak student to succeed, or when one of your students tells you just what you mean to them. It is a rare and very special job that can offer you all this and more.

Appendix: Contact Addresses and Telephone Numbers for Teaching Unions

The Association of Teachers and Lecturers
7 Northumberland Street
London WC2N 5DA
Telephone: (0171) 930 6441

The National Association of Schoolmasters and Union of Women Teachers
Hillscourt Education Centre
Rose Hill
Rednal
Birmingham B45 8RS
Telephone: (0121) 453 6150

The National Union of Teachers
Hamilton House
Mabledon Place
London WC1H 9BD
Telephone: (0171) 388 6191

The Professional Association of Teachers
2 St. James' Court
Friar Gate
Derby DE1 1BT
Telephone: (01332) 372337

Index